CLEAR!

Living the Life You Didn't Dream Of

Dear James,

Live & love with kindness.

Best,

Herman J. Williams, MD

For more information about this title or to order other books
and/or electronic media, contact the publisher:

Atkins & Greenspan Writing
18530 Mack Avenue, Suite 166
Grosse Pointe Farms, MI 48236
www.atkinsgreenspan.com

ISBN:
978-1-945875-16-8 (Hardcover)
978-1-945875-14-4 (Paperback)
978-1-945875-15-1 (eBook)

Printed in the United States of America

Cover and Interior design: Van-garde Imagery

"Herman Williams' story of survival and triumph in the face of repeated medical crises will leave the reader inspired to tackle his or her own life challenges. CLEAR! demonstrates that with faith and determination, anything is possible."

Bill Frist, MD
Former U.S. Senate Majority Leader

"This gripping, inspirational story of the triumph of the human spirit by a superb physician, leader, family man, and healthcare executive reminds in vivid detail that our lives are never to be taken for granted. A story nothing short of remarkable is characterized by grit, love, perseverance and faith."

Wayne J. Riley, MD, MPH, MBA, MACP
President, SUNY Brooklyn Downstate Medical Center
President Emeritus, American College of Physicians

"This very impressive narrative about Herman's resilience is a love story with a great message that will embolden people to get up, try again, and commit to helping others. It's extremely inspiring."

Dr. Augustus White
Harvard Medical School

Contents

Dedication

I DEDICATE THIS BOOK to my sister Janet, who died at age 31, too soon before she could make her mark on this great world. I also dedicate this book to my father, for being the role model every young man should have, and for the generosity, love, and support that he shared with me until his death in 2011.

Acknowledgements

I WANT TO ACKNOWLEDGE Elizabeth Ann Atkins for her incredible writing and vision for bringing my life experience to paper, and Catherine M. Greenspan for publishing the book. To Richard Manson, for acting as creative advisor for the book, and providing time to review and mold the story. To Don Parks, Gus White, Hugh Greeley, Kent Wallace, and Richard Williams for mentoring me over my lifetime. Special thanks to William Lionel Daley, for personally monitoring my treatment regimens, always being by my side, and being the brother I never had. To Phil Morris, for being my hero and never-ending friend. Phil has understood everything I have gone through, and he has especially helped me see my way to my true purpose in life. To my mom, for her support, love, and guidance over the past 58 years. To my son, Cole, for becoming the compassionate man embodied in the book, and for being a blessing from God. To my dearest wife, Jeannie, for never leaving my side, being my coach, walking with me through hell and back, and staying my wife for the last 26 years.

First Foreword

WITH TONGUE IN CHEEK, I advise the readers of this book to prepare to be SHOCKED. This is a small book that delivers a real punch to the heart as well as to the psyche. It deals with very intense physical pain as well as with the raw, emotional ordeal suffered by the protagonist and author, Herman Williams, MD, in this real-life drama.

In this Foreword, I will not attempt to reenact the awesome details that are laid out in a very intriguing fashion about the life, death, and resuscitation of my dear friend Herman, who suffered more internal abuse than anyone still living whom I have ever known. Instead, I will briefly give you my reaction to the book from the perspective of someone who is familiar with the subject of sudden cardiac death *and* who also knows the individual who was the victim of this literally life-and-death situation in which his own body seemed to have turned against him.

I happen to be a cardiologist on the faculty of the UCLA School of Medicine in Los Angeles, where I am also a Professor of Medicine. That is where I first met Herman. He came to my office many years ago seeking advice about how to get into medical school. I took an immediate liking to him, not only because he had the same last name as I do and was of my race, but also because of his engaging personality. He is the kind of person you would have to deliberately work hard not to like: a tall, handsome, slender, athletic, African American young man, with a great smile and a down-to-earth, laid-back manner. His conversation when we met was easy-going, but I had no doubt about his determination to become a doctor, despite being rebuffed on his initial attempt.

As a member of UCLA's medical school Admissions Committee and as one who had previously served in that same capacity at Harvard Medical School, I was used to sizing up prospective candidates to ascertain if they had the right stuff, and to determine if they were what I call the real deal: well-prepared, serious with honest motivation, dedicated to purpose, and with the proven mental and physical ability to withstand the rigors of years of monastic study. I had the sense that he possessed these ingredients, but he had some academic issues.

I agreed to become a sort of long-distance mentor for him. He was able to combine my advice with further advice from medical icons such as Dr. Donald Parks, Dr. Clarence Shields, and my old friend, Dr. Augustus White. Ultimately, Herman achieved his goal of gaining entrance to medical school at Boston University. Later, when he was in his Orthopedics residency at the University of Washington, he arranged for me to come to his institution to give a lecture on a subject I had done considerable research on and eventually written a book about: sudden cardiac death –– *The Athlete and Heart Disease*, Lippincott, 1999. Perhaps that was a prophetic visit, because later Herman had his life-altering experience with sudden death.

It is said that there is nothing more devastating to the human body than a heart attack. Although that is not exactly what Herman had, his cardiac condition (which no one knew lurked within him) is a rare congenital condition called Right Ventricular Dysplasia. It can cause the same result that a heart attack often does, which is sudden death. When Herman had his episode, he was fortunate to have two things in his favor that made the difference between permanent death and survival: being in the presence of his fellow residents who gave him CPR; and having his family, especially his incredible wife Jeannie and his devoted father, who became a formidable support group that literally would not let him die.

His survival against unbelievable odds, without a doubt, was due to a great extent to his own tremendous resolve not to give up or give in. His determination is the epitome of the famous poem by Dylan Thomas that exhorted people who face seemingly irreversible life-threatening circumstances to resist and to press onward:

Do not go gentle into that good night.
Rage, rage against the dying of the light.

But, of course, he also had God on his side. How else could you explain the fact that he dodged so many bullets?

This question of whether there was a divine role in all that Herman was exposed to is at the crux of the issue, and may even be called "the heart of the matter." Allow me to explain. Toward the end of the book, Herman reveals that he had an epiphany, which may be translated as a *Eureka!* moment or, "Now I can see what this is all about." This is when he indicated that he now understood that he had been selected to be an instrument of God; to show how one can suffer nearly to the point of death and yet recover to do God's work of lifting up the downtrodden. God was showing him that there was a higher purpose for him, rather than just limiting him to fixing backs and repairing bones. And indeed, that is what he has become: a doctor, not of orthopedics, but a healer of souls and spirits who helps to eliminate healthcare disparities in his role as a top physician executive with one of the foremost healthcare providers in the country. I hope that I do not seem to be too imaginative to suggest that Herman had a few angels who guided the transformation of his career from orthopedics into a field where he has had a much wider impact on people.

So, I urge the reader to look beyond the morbid details of the drama that absorbed the life of Herman Williams, MD, and recognize the fact that he has been transformed into a man who has answered a higher calling. We can all thank God for making that possible, although Herman may want to ask God, "Did it have to hurt so much to accomplish this?" The answer is that only the Divine One knows. Meanwhile, the public that Herman serves is the beneficiary of his dedicated service. For that, we are all truly blessed to have such a specially gifted physician and humanitarian still walking among us. I hope that his tenure is a long one.

Richard Allen Williams, MD, FACC, FAHA, FACP
117th President, National Medical Association
Clinical Professor of Medicine, UCLA School of Medicine
Founder, Association of Black Cardiologists
Los Angeles, California

Second Foreword

Our fast-paced, high-tech world is becoming so imper-
sonal, that sometimes we forget to look people in the eye, say thank
you, and share the niceties that lighten the day.

We become disconnected from others and the noise of our mod-
ern-day reality — with devices pinging, ringing, streaming, and flash-
ing around the clock. This robs us of the calm and quiet required to
center ourselves. As a result, we lose focus with who we really are. And
that plunges us into a fog of fear, anxiety, and even depression.

CLEAR! Living the Life You Didn't Dream Of by Herman J.
Williams, MD, is the antidote. This book enables you to find clarity
in the chaos of life, especially if you are going through a catastrophic
challenge such as illness, death of a loved one, financial problems, job
loss, or an injury.

My dear friend and protégé Herman Williams, MD, bares his soul
on these pages, and believe me, it is one of the purest souls you will
ever encounter. These written words flow with the same peaceful,
soothing energy that radiates from him when he enters a room. His
presence is as kind and calming as his voice, making him a conciliator
extraordinaire in business and social settings.

I felt that immediately when we met years ago.

You will feel this as you immerse yourself in his heart-wrenching and courageous story. It was through his suffering that Herman discovered his true purpose in life. While his dream of becoming a healer in the form of an orthopedic surgeon literally died with his body 26 years ago, his destiny was reborn with a bigger and broader purpose for his life. Now he is a healer on a far grander scale, through his daily work as a hospital administrator, and as the author of this book.

You are holding in your hands a blueprint for finding purpose in your pain, as well as tools to make a powerful impact on the world, through the simplest interactions with others throughout your day.

So, if you really want to delve into the depths of understanding who you are and how you might lead people in your life, this is the book you want to read.

It challenges you to look inside, for all of the answers to living your best life are within you. Only there can you focus through the fog and find the clarity you need for better health, prosperity, love, and peace.

Richard Manson
CEO
SourceMark LLC

Preface

DEAR READERS:

You are about to hear the sincere ramblings of a very proud mother. I was blessed with two wonderful children and a loving, attentive husband. Though we were Southerners, my husband and I brought our values and beliefs to the West Coast.

Herman Joseph comes from a tight-knit group of relatives and friends who always wanted the best for each other and who were continual cheerleaders for one another. We demonstrated and practiced principles that included love of family, love of God, respect for elders, service to community, humility, and gratitude.

We viewed education as a key to success. Our immediate neighborhood was populated by educated and/or professional people. We were very involved in our children's schools and took advantage of all that was available to them there, including the arts.

As a youngster, Herman was easygoing, friendly, and outgoing. He loved music, and actively cultivates that interest to this day. His average performance in grade school offered few clues that he would pursue medicine or become successful in that field. At the time, he did not display the drive or fervor required for such a rigorous occupation. Was I ever WRONG! Once he decided on a medical career, he gave it his all. I was totally awed — and extremely proud!

Having grown up in the segregated South, I triumphed over discrimination and harassment as I earned my education and embarked on a long, robust career as a psychiatric social worker. All the while, my husband and I instilled in Herman a strong sense of self, justice, and tenacity to do what is right.

Now, as the lone survivors of our nuclear family, Herman and I are extremely close. He knows who I am, as well as what I need and want. With the passing of time, our roles have reversed, as he has become my protector. I love him even more for assuming this role and helping me to maintain as much independence as possible, especially after his father's death.

Even so, reading his book has deepened my understanding and enlightenment about my son. Prior to this, I was not privy to the extent of the psychological and physical pain that he has endured because of his medical condition. He has experienced gigantic highs, painful disappointments, and devastating lows while fighting to regain an acceptable level of stability and function.

His loving wife, Jeannie, and their son, Cole, have been a source of strength and support for him, and I thank God for them. I am also grateful that he has maintained contact with a cadre of delightful, loyal friends over many years. Through it all, he has emerged as a wonderful human being and a beacon of hope for many. He is patient, understanding, thoughtful, calm, supportive, friendly, and still one of the most easy-going people I have ever known. Oh, yes, I am totally subjective, but if you meet him, you will quickly know I am right!

Gabrielle Williams
The Proud Mother

Introduction

"The starting point of great success and achievement has always been the same. It is for you to 'dream big dreams.' There is nothing more important, and nothing that works faster, than for you to cast off your own limitations and begin dreaming and fantasizing about the wonderful things that you can become and have and do."[1]

Brian Tracy
Author
The Psychology of Achievement

WHAT IF YOU DID all the above, starting as a child, and began living the life of your dreams — but suddenly lost it all?

Would you wallow in self-pity and give up?

Or would you create a new dream and a life that you could enjoy?

Tragic circumstances forced me to answer these questions 26 years ago when death literally killed my dream.

I had diligently followed Brian Tracy's guidance to dream my own big dream of becoming one of the top orthopedic surgeons in

---

1   http://www.briantracy.com/blog/personal-success/dream-big-live-your-life-without-limits/ Brian Tracy is recognized as the top sales training and personal success authority in the world today. He has authored more than 60 books and has produced more than 500 audio and video learning programs on sales, management, business success, and personal development, including worldwide bestseller *The Psychology of Achievement*. Brian's goal is to help you achieve your personal and business goals faster and easier than you ever imagined.

Los Angeles and caring for superstar athletes who entertained and inspired people everywhere. Perhaps my dream was as materialistic as it was altruistic, but nevertheless, I set a huge goal for my life, and began working to attain it at an early age. Many dominoes fell into place, from selecting my high school and college, to getting into medical school, and pursuing one of the most difficult surgical subspecialties in medicine.

By age 31, I was so close to achieving my dream, I could taste it. But then something crazy and unexpected happened...

And it thrust me into an agonizing situation that propelled me to a crossroads where I had a choice: spiral down a miserable exit ramp to permanent despair, or ascend to a new dimension and behold spectacular new vistas for my life. This fork in the road inspired spiritual contemplation. Something deep within me came alive, and my intuitive inner voice revealed that the key to thriving despite any circumstances is that:

> *You must embrace and acknowledge where you are, accept the conditions around you, and decide that you will make a difference in your life and the lives of others.*

In that moment, I suddenly understood where and who I was, and what the consequences were. I realized that I had options: to stay depressed, or to transform my tragedy into something positive to help other people in a big way.

"I am a survivor!" I declared. "And neither my story nor my suffering will go to waste." It has been my test. It is now my testimony to inspire you to choose the upward path when your world crumbles and leaves you whimpering at a difficult intersection where you have to make tough choices.

No one's future is guaranteed. But my new daily reality birthed an awakening to a life that brings me indescribable joy and gratitude all day, every day.

As a result, I was moved to revisit Brian Tracy's directive, which prompted me to dream a new dream that is bigger and better in many ways than my original one. At the core of this dream lies the personal *Mission Statement* that was borne of my unforeseen ordeal. Now it has become my passion and purpose to execute this mission that says, simply:

My reason for living is to make sure that everyone I encounter is better off when they leave me.

Whether that improves another person's day by giving them a smile, or opening a door for someone, or making a special call for a patient to a physician to clarify a health concern, or any one of numerous other gestures of compassion, I conduct these acts with every person I encounter on a daily basis. The new dream reaches my professional life as an executive in a national healthcare company. I never realized that this position would enable me to help exponentially more people than the one-on-one impact that I would have had as a surgeon.

Exactly what steps did I take to embark upon this journey to create and achieve a new dream? The answers lie on the pages of this book. I am sharing them with you, so that you may enjoy life more fully on every level — without having to experience the fear that wrenched these lessons from deep within me.

So, if tragedy or circumstances have changed your dreams along the way, here is my "how-to" formula for living a new life you didn't dream of — with grace, gratitude, and immense pleasure every day.

Sincerely,

Herman J. Williams, MD, MBA, MPH

Chapter One

The First Dream

As the alarm blares at 4:30 in the morning, it's more jarring than usual, because I am already awake. My beautiful wife is sleeping peacefully beside me. She hasn't moved since I rose two hours earlier to carry out my increasingly frequent middle-of-the-night pee. I inevitably return to bed and lie wide-eyed as my brain flashes with the fantastical moments I envision myself having throughout the day at work, and later with my wife and our friends. The house is silent, except for the steady rhythm of waves crashing on the beach below our bedroom balcony. I stretch, drawing the salty, exhilarating ocean air deep into my lungs.

Ding!

The coffee pot in the kitchen spurs me to action like the pistol at my high school track meets where I always sprinted to victory. Now, as the scent of fresh-brewed coffee wafts into the room, my mouth waters. I can't wait to taste that first hot, creamy sip. But first, I jump into the shower, where I shave, brush my teeth, and bask under the soft droplets of warm water.

Minutes later, I'm dressed in my favorite suit — green surgery scrubs. In the kitchen, I savor my cup of coffee. As the caffeine accelerates my thoughts, I tick down my list of surgeries for the day:

- Anterior cruciate ligament repair of the right knee — for the starting guard for the Los Angeles Lakers.

- Repair of the right patellar ligament — Mr. Jones.

- Examination under anesthesia with soft tissue release of the right shoulder, possible rotator cuff repair — Ms. Chapman.

Details of each procedure whiz through my head as I hop into my Porsche. As I maneuver through LA's notorious traffic, I can't get to work soon enough to live another day of my dream as an accomplished, hard-working surgeon.

While growing up in the middle-class enclave of Windsor Hills, and having been granted an out-of-area permit to attend Beverly Hills High School, my childhood and teen years had convinced me that if I worked hard enough, the sky would be the limit... if I made all the right moves.

While driving, I smile, remembering how my dad had frequently painted a picture of my future as the quintessential "Renaissance Man" — a well-educated physician and musician.

Yes, I have truly become that.

My car phone rings. It's internationally known orthopedic surgeon Augustus A. White, III, the first African American department chief at Harvard's teaching hospital. He and famed orthopedic surgeon Clarence L. Shields, MD, had become my mentors during medical school.

"Herman," Gus says, "Clarence and I will be in town next week for the Academy of Orthopedic Surgeons meeting, and we would like to take you to dinner to check on you."

"Gus, great things are happening for me," I say proudly. "You won't be disappointed."

Dr. White had been instrumental in my success, having given me the opportunity to publish in the peer-reviewed journal, *SPINE*. My successful Fellowship in Sports Medicine at the Kerlan-Jobe Orthopaedic Clinic in Los Angeles — where Dr. Shields trained me — had catapulted me into my dream job.

I had fantasized about this life since childhood, while hanging out after school in my mom's mental health clinic, as she finished her day as a psychiatric social worker. After graduating with honors from high school, I earned my bachelor's degree from Amherst College, and my MD from Boston University School of Medicine, along with a Master's in Public Health from Harvard University. These accomplishments required more than a decade of diligent, difficult work. Each served as a solid brick in the foundation of my dream that had brought me to this moment.

"Good morning, Dr. Williams." Doctors, nurses, and other hospital staff greet me as I stride confidently through the doors to the Intensive Care Unit. I put on my white doctor's coat embroidered over my heart with HERMAN WILLIAMS, MD, ORTHOPEDIC SURGEON, and I begin doing rounds (or "rounding" as we call it) on the most seriously ill patients.

"Yes, it is a very good morning," I respond as a cardiac monitor pierces my ears with its faint, steady *beep…beep…beep…beep.*

Here in my first patient's room, I'm struck by the sterile and pungent smell of medicine and sickness. The man is lying still in bed, surrounded by a bank of machines that blink with red and green lights. His heartbeat streams in a zig-zag across the screen of the EKG machine. I stand near the foot of the bed, glancing at his chart.

"Herman," a soft voice says as the beeping grows louder.

I look around, but can't see who's calling my name.

"Herman!"

Everything blurs, then comes into focus. I realize that I am not seeing the monitors, hearing the beeps, or inhaling the hospital smells from my usual perspective as the patient's surgeon.

Because I am the man in the bed.

My God! I'm the patient!

And I'm in the ICU.

"Herman, it's time for your morning vitals," says the voice that had been calling my name.

Suddenly I remember: *One week ago, I died!*

Doctors had resuscitated me. And now I'm waking up to a nightmare.

CHAPTER TWO

My Death

IF YOU WERE STRANDED on a desert island, which type of physician would you take with you?

"I'd take a gastroenterologist," some might respond, "because if you get dysentery, they would be ideal to treat you."

Another might answer, "Take an orthopedic surgeon, because you'll undoubtedly succumb to a musculoskeletal injury and need someone who can treat those injuries."

Me? I'd choose an anesthesiologist. They have great gases, they're good conversationalists, and if you ever have a cardiac arrest, they can perform CPR and "tube you" if necessary.

> *One week before I awoke from that dream in the ICU, the events preceding my death began as Jeannie and I enjoyed what seemed like an ordinary day. Here's what happened...*

Dewdrops on the lush green grass and trees sparkled like a million tiny diamonds as the sun made a rare and glorious appearance in Seattle, Washington.

"What a gorgeous day," I said, glancing at my beautiful fiancée as we drove north to look at a house that was for sale. "I'll take all this sunshine as a good omen for my day off from the hospital."

Jeannie playfully responded, "Enjoy it while it's here, because we only get a few days of sunshine in a year."

It was a well-known fact for folks who live in the Pacific Northwest that the sun only broke through the gloomy rainclouds 50 of every 365 days.

"All that rain," I said, admiring the verdant palette shrouding the road, "gives us all this beauty. And allow me to be totally cliché, and say the rainbow doesn't appear until *after* the storm."

Jeannie laughed and squeezed my hand. An electrifying ripple shot through me. I was so blessed that such a sweet, caring woman wanted to spend the rest of her life with me. We first met in her native Boston, when I was a medical student. One look at her long, dark hair and sparkling eyes, and I was in love. At the time, we were both in relationships, and I dreamed of one day being her boyfriend.

That magic moment finally happened one year later, when we were both single. I saw her again, as she was working in the dental school. We dated for two years until finally (in March of 1990) I honored the tradition of asking her father if I could marry her. He said yes, blessing me with a partner to build a future. She made me laugh, and her passionate spirit connected with mine in a visceral way that left no doubt. She was my soul mate.

Now, on this sunny Seattle day, I couldn't wait to return to Boston for our wedding in five months. The celebration would include Jeannie's huge family. And I was grateful that my best childhood friend, Phil Morris, would leave whatever film or television set where he was working as an actor in L.A. to stand as my best man, and that my "brother," Dr. William "Bill" Daley, would put his work as a cardiologist on hold for a day to serve as one of my groomsmen. Jeannie and I planned to celebrate our honeymoon on the Caribbean island of St. Maarten. After that, Jeannie and I looked forward to our second wedding reception with my family in L.A., and a third celebration in Seattle with our friends.

On April 28, 1991, my life seemed perfect. I felt so on track toward achieving my dream life that I could taste it. At the time, my goal was twofold: to emulate my parents' passion for helping people, which they achieved as psychiatric social workers; and to be a great orthopedic surgeon in Los Angeles. With Jeannie at my side, I would do this by becoming an orthopedic surgeon specializing in sports medicine, taking care of celebrity athletes who played for teams such as the Lakers and the Rams. This prestigious position promised to deliver me to my definition of success, given that I had already rotated as a medical student -- and had been mentored by -- Clarence Shields, MD, in the Kerlan-Jobe sports medicine practice.

All I needed was to complete my orthopedic surgery residency at America's fifth best trauma program at the University of Washington in Seattle. After that, I would apply for a fellowship in sports medicine with the Kerlan Clinic in Los Angeles. And that would propel my dream into our reality.

This could not come soon enough, because my residency had become extremely stressful. The first two years were grueling, as I became acclimated to the demanding pace of the only Level I Trauma Center serving Washington, Alaska, Montana, and Idaho. Paramedics trained there, and thanks to the Seattle Fire Department pioneering the nation's first Medic One program 21 years earlier, Seattle was leading the nation in saving lives with CPR.

Correspondent Morley Safer had once said on *60 Minutes,* "If you have to have a heart attack, have it in Seattle," during a report praising Seattle's Medic One Program and the subsequent high survival rate for heart attack victims. Needless to say, my fellow residents and I were meticulously trained in Cardio Pulmonary Resuscitation (CPR), and we put our skills to use by saving lives every day.

The residency program was exhilarating, but exhausting. I was often on call every other night — back before an eight-hour break was mandated for residents between shifts. Although challenging, I made my mark in the program as a genuine contributor.

Unfortunately, things started to crumble during my third year, when one attending physician, whose responsibilities included supervising, teaching, and training residents, tormented me with a Dr. Jekyll-Mr. Hyde disposition. He was fun when he joined us after work for a beer. Back in the hospital, however, where his role as the attending physician was to pass the torch of our trade as an art to us residents, he was always changing directions on me. For example, he would tell me to change a patient's wound dressing, only to later chastise me for doing so, as if he'd never given the order.

He was never satisfied. In retrospect, I don't believe it was a race issue. However, as only the second African American in the program's history, I wondered if he thought I didn't belong. One day, he was belittling me and began speaking in an unprofessional way. I finally looked him square in the eye, and said, "I am not a child! I am a grown man, and I will not allow you to treat me this way."

I immediately met with my chairman, who sided with me and agreed to speak to my attending. I was so proud of myself for not letting anything get in my way. Dammit, I was going to succeed at being an accomplished orthopedic surgeon — or die trying.

Oops, did I say that too loud?

My heart had been racing with frightening episodes of irregular heartbeats accompanied by dizziness for the previous six or eight months.

Had the stress of dealing with my attending physician damaged my body? Was something wrong with my heart?

That question would scare anyone, but for me, it was especially chilling. A brain aneurysm had stolen my sister Janet's life eight years earlier, when she was only 31 years old.

Ironically, I was now 31, physically fit, and the apparent picture of health. But Janet's early death roused the grim and relentless fear that I, too, might have an unfortunate genetic predisposition to other connective tissue ailments. As a result, my parents and Jeannie shared the question that haunted me day and night:

Is my heart a ticking time bomb that could obliterate my life in a heartbeat?

Anxiety about my heart only exacerbated the bad feeling that was creeping over me as Jeannie and I drove farther northward into desolate, unknown territory.

"I don't like where we're headed," I said. "Why are we even looking for a house in a town that's known for its devout KKK residents?"

A fearful chill silenced us as I remembered why we were even going there. That morning I'd spoken with my mother, who still lived in my childhood home in Windsor Hills.

"Herman Joseph," she'd said, "your father and I want you and Jeannie to go look at a house this morning. Your condo in Seattle is too small. Can you do that for us?"

"Of course, Mom," I had answered, grateful to share such a close relationship with my parents. They had purchased properties in the cities where I attended college and medical school to facilitate their frequent visits. Forever changed by the pain of losing their daughter, they worried about my health and wanted to be near me.

My mother had continued, "Today we're going shopping to look for my dress for your wedding. Let us know what you think of the house and the town it's in."

Jeannie and I looked around, and I said, "I haven't seen a person of color for the last 10 miles. That is not a good sign."

Our apprehensive silence spun me deeper into worry about my irregular heartbeat, which had prompted me to seek an evaluation from a cardiologist. Since I'm a physician, the doctor gave me the proverbial million-dollar work-up that included a stress test, a cardiac monitor that I wore for two weeks, and a cardiac echocardiogram.

"We found nothing irregular," the doctor had said, "although you do have idiopathic tachycardia." Translation: *rapid heart rate of unknown origin*. However, my cardiologist elected not to place me on antiarrhythmic medication that could decrease the number of irregular beats.

"The side effects from the medication would be worse than the symptoms from your irregular heartbeats," she'd said. "Herman, I know you like to enjoy your mochas every day, but you need to stop drinking coffee and all caffeinated drinks. If your symptoms become worse, call me right away."

This clean bill of health was a green light to continue my residency training, as well as my commitment to physical fitness. Having played high school football, I now maintained my slim, muscular physique by playing as much high-energy, smack-talking intramural basketball with my fellow residents as possible. Our hectic schedules left little time for it, so we seized every opportunity to play with gusto.

"Jeannie, are you ready for this?" I asked to distract us both from worry as we drove through unfamiliar, slightly uncomfortable surroundings. "Today is the official showdown between the Anesthesia Residents and the Neurosurgery Residents. It could get rough out there on the court."

"Are you feeling up to it?" Jeannie asked, still worried about my recent health concern. Though she had switched her career focus to become a dental hygienist, she had attended nursing school for a short period, and remained a nurse at heart.

A triple-whammy of circumstances had changed her career course: unnecessary remarks from a nursing school instructor that made her feel inadequate; a break-up with her high school boyfriend; and her grandmother's death. After that, she attended the Forsyth School of Dental Hygienists in Boston. One year into the two-year program, Jeannie and I started dating. Jeannie graduated from Forsyth in June of 1989, and I left for my residency in Seattle later that month. In March of 1990, I asked Jeannie to marry me over the phone. In May of 1990, Jeannie moved to Seattle. That summer, she started a program to prepare her for the Washington state board examination. While waiting to take the board examination, she worked at a dental office as an assistant. Now, she cast a concerned look at me as we drove in search of this property for my parents.

"I'm fine," I said, "but I'll be better after looking at this house."

But once there, we immediately agreed that it was not our style.

"Let's get out of here!" I said, shifting down into second gear to turn around. "We don't want to turn a corner and accidentally run into a KKK parade."

Little did we know that the relief of fleeing the unknown and speeding back to our comfort zone would ironically catapult us closer to the most horrifying experience of our lives.

"Hey, Herman's here!" announced Glenn, an anesthesia resident and a very close friend as Jeannie and I entered the gymnasium at Seattle's Ravenna-Eckstein Community Center. "Jeannie, how's it going?"

"I'm great!" she said. "How are you, Glenn?"

I didn't know it in that moment, but I had made two of the best decisions of my life: bringing my soon-to-be wife to this basketball game, and playing with a bunch of anesthesiologists, who greeted us both with big, welcoming smiles.

We were a close-knit group. The pressures of our residency programs forged strong bonds, and we leaned on each other for moral support and encouragement. Together we had endured the heavy-duty component of trauma training that included responding to our specialty call in the emergency room. We handled all kinds of life-and-death crises, and got to know most of the paramedics in town when they brought in victims of car accidents, shootings, heart attacks, and other catastrophic events.

We also cherished the fact that our individual success depended on teamwork. Just as a baseball player cannot play baseball without a bat, a surgeon cannot perform surgery without an anesthesiologist. Many of my friends were anesthesiologists, and they drafted me onto their basketball team. I was about to join four anesthesiologists playing against five neurosurgical residents.

I was excited, but Jeannie looked worried. "Herman, are you sure you're feeling up to this?"

"I'm fine," I said, telling myself I was the picture of health despite the recent episodes of dizziness and racing heartbeat.

The game began at noon, and we played hard, as our gym shoes screeched on the wooden floor. On the sidelines, Jeannie was keeping score with Val, whose husband, Todd, was running up and down the court with me.

Suddenly, I felt dizzy. Light-headed. Nauseous. I left the game and sat on a bench about 15 feet from Jeannie. She was looking back and forth between me and the players.

I made a throaty, choking sound. Then I slumped over, foaming at the mouth. My body was angled in a weird position, and I started to slide down off the bench.

Jeannie ran toward me.

"Glenn!" she screamed. But the guys didn't hear her over the noise in the gym. "Glenn! Glenn!"

My friend, Dr. A. (who prefers to remain anonymous because he says he simply did what a physician is trained to do) was running down the court when he heard Jeannie scream. Then he saw me, slumped in an awkward position, with my arms limp by my sides. For Jeannie, consumed by panic, the guys appeared to be running toward us in slow motion. My friends grabbed me, laid me flat on the floor, and ripped off my shirt.

"No pulse!" Dr. A. announced.

Another doc exclaimed, "He's not breathing!"

A third said, "Pupils dilated. Rapidly becoming cyanotic."

It was 1:15 p.m., and I was dead. I did not "see the light" or experience any mystical sightings of angels or deceased loved ones. I heard nothing. My brain recorded no memory of being dead.

"Holy crap!" Dr. A. exclaimed. "This is Herman! Let's start CPR!" He started mouth-to-mouth resuscitation. The other doctors performed chest compressions.

Glenn ran to a pay phone to call 911. Cell phones had just become affordable and only a few residents had one. Jeannie and Val went to the lobby to await the paramedics' arrival. Jeannie was probably thinking, *Oh my God, this is it!*

Today, cardiac arrest kills more than 90 percent of the victims it strikes outside of a hospital, and 75 percent of those who are patients in the hospital, according to the American Heart Association's 2013 statistics. Imagine the stats for 1991!

As every second ticked by, the odds were dramatically and increasingly stacking against me. Starting three minutes after cardiac arrest, irreversible brain damage and tissue damage begin to occur. For every minute thereafter, until a defibrillator is used to deliver an electric shock to re-start the heart, chances of survival decrease by seven percent. After that, the rate of survival decreases 10 percent every minute!

As my doctor friends performed textbook-perfect CPR, they understood these facts better than anyone. They manually pumped my heart by delivering quick compressions on my sternum. This action kept my blood circulating to nourish my brain and tissues, along with the oxygen that Dr. A. was blowing into my lungs. Ideally, CPR should kick-start a heartbeat and get the lungs pumping. Dr. A. became ticked off because I did not start breathing and had no pulse.

"Come on, man!" he exclaimed.

My attempts to imagine the horrified thoughts haranguing my friends, bring to mind a famous line from the great satirical novel, *The House of God*, by Samuel Shem, MD. In it, the protagonist recounts his fictional residency training at Boston's Beth Israel Hospital during the 1970s. His third law of *The House of God* is: "At a cardiac arrest, the first procedure is to take your own pulse."[1]

---

1   Samuels, Shem. *The House of God*. Berkeley. (Original work published 1978).

My friends must have thought, *Here is our buddy Herman, a fellow resident,* while our training must have been spinning in their heads:

- *Time is muscle… the longer it takes to resuscitate a person, the more damage to the heart muscle…*

- *Cardiac arrest outside the hospital has the least chance of survival…*

- *Pupils dilated suggests that even if we resuscitate him, he will probably have permanent brain damage…*

- *Shit! Don't think. Just keep compressions and breaths coming!*

After 10 minutes of CPR, Dr. A. was wondering, *What's taking the Medic One boys so long to arrive?* Jeannie, still waiting in the lobby, was asking the same question.

Statistically speaking, my prognosis was grim. Yet my friends did not give up.

"I hear sirens!" Jeannie exclaimed to Val.

The ambulance finally arrived. As the Emergency Medical Technicians or EMTs rushed into the gym with a defibrillator, a surreal moment occurred as the medics and doctors recognized each other. These two teams usually met in the ER. Now, when the paramedics saw me lying dead on the floor, they realized: *The man on the floor is Dr. Herman Williams, the trauma orthopedic resident at Harborview Hospital who has greeted us countless times when we brought patients to the ER.*

"We'll take over from here, guys," one medic told my friends.

They stepped back as the EMTs prepared to jumpstart my heartbeat with a defibrillator. It contains a portable battery attached via cords to two paddles that were supposed to deliver 200 joules of electric current to shock my heart, just as jumper cables can re-start a car battery. One paramedic spread gel on my bare chest, then another pressed one paddle above my heart and the other below it.

I have often imagined that the EMT declared, "I love this part!" before he exclaimed:

"CLEAR!"

His command warned everyone to step back from my body. Otherwise, they risked getting an electric shock as the defibrillator would, when activated, powerfully jolt my body and make it jerk up violently, as countless TV shows have depicted. A deep buzzing sound would also accompany the life-giving electricity that was surging through my body.

But not this time.

The gym remained silent.

And my body was still.

The doctors and medics paused.

Wait a minute. There is not supposed to be a pause!

"The paddles are not working!" the EMT exclaimed with a shocked tone.

Oh, my God, the paddles are not working. You have got to be kidding me! Guys, don't just stand there. Resume CPR!

Like magic, my buddies jumped down to continue chest compressions and mouth-to-mouth.

Meanwhile, Jeannie's hopeful relief turned to panic. She was still in the lobby, and had heard someone say the defibrillator was not working. For her, it seemed like a year before the Seattle Fire Department's Medic One ambulance arrived. The paramedics ran into the gym with a new defibrillator.

It worked!

"He's got a pulse!" they shouted.

Amazingly, the residents had performed more than 10 minutes of CPR on me. Once I had a pulse, they took over what was typically the medics' job. My friends intubated me by placing a tube down my windpipe to help me breathe. And despite the extremely unsterile conditions, they inserted a "central line" catheter into a large vein in my neck that facilitated immediate delivery of life-saving fluids and medications into my body.

I had entered the gym on the verge of living my dream. Now I was being wheeled out on a gurney, unconscious, and totally unaware that in one fateful heartbeat — or technically, lack thereof — death had killed my dream.

CHAPTER THREE

The Doctor Is Now A Patient
aka Steven Seagal

"Harborview ER, this is Medic One," the medic said into the radio to announce the next arrival into the Emergency Department. "We have a 31-year-old Black male who has sustained an out-of-hospital cardiac arrest. We discovered him with compressions ongoing at the scene. He was ultimately defibrillated into sinus rhythm, but is now in ventricular tachycardia, is tubed, and unconscious. We will arrive in the ED in five minutes."

MY COLLEAGUES' JAWS DROPPED in shock as they watched the paramedics wheel me through those emergency room doors. I was unconscious and cyanotic: my skin appeared blue-purple due to lack of oxygen. Tubes extended down my throat and protruded from my neck. They rushed me into the Medical Intensive Care Unit (MICU) for observation and tests.

Meanwhile, Jeannie rode to the hospital with Todd and Val because she was unable to drive my car's stick shift. The three of them were confined to a small waiting room while doctors evaluated me. Todd was in shock. Jeannie was terrified. And she panicked at the thought of telling my parents that this happened to their only surviving child, who was the same age as my sister when she died. She calmed down enough to call my father and tell him what she knew, which was very little because she had not seen me since arriving at the hospital.

Dad called my brother-like friend, Bill, hoping to receive from him some answers, because Bill was a cardiologist. Meanwhile, Mom booked a flight for Dad from Los Angeles to Seattle. But my father was not going to wait to catch a plane.

"Cancel the flight," he said. "I'm driving."

"I can't go with you," Mom told him. As the Clinical Program Director for the Los Angeles County Jail's 35-bed inpatient psychiatric ward, my mother's responsibility was tremendous. "I need to go to work to straighten things out. I can't leave until I arrange proper coverage in my absence."

With that, my father prepared to leave for Seattle.

About six hours later, Jeannie was finally allowed into the MICU to visit me.

"Oh, my God!" she cried, staring in shock at my motionless body, which was hooked up to anything and everything that could connect to a tube. One snaked into my mouth and down my throat to help me breathe. Jutting from my neck was a central line, which allowed for the drawing of blood, the delivery of nutrients, and the insertion of a catheter to my heart. Clips extended from my fingertips to measure the oxygen level in my blood.

A constant *beep... beep... beep!* screamed from the multitude of monitors around my bed.

Meanwhile, Jeannie's nursing training made her acutely aware that people resuscitated from sudden death often suffered brain damage.

Jeannie had previously enrolled in a nursing program, but eventually realized her professional career path was elsewhere. All she could think was, *Oh my God, is he going to remember me? Does he know we're going to get married in five months?*

Our close friends, Doug and Sue, joined Jeannie in my room. They just watched me and prayed for a miracle.

Suddenly, my eyes opened. I gagged. The horrible sensation of hot, sour puke spewed up and around my breathing tube. I gagged again, drawing vomit into my lungs. After a struggle, my nurse pulled out the tube. Then I focused on the people in the room.

"Jeannie!" I exclaimed.

"Oh my God, yes!" She sighed tearfully.

"What happened?" I asked.

"Honey, you had a cardiac arrest," she said. "You went down during the basketball game. The residents resuscitated you. You're in the ICU."

My expression conveyed that I understood, as she and our friends shared more details. When they finished, I asked, "What happened?"

They described the incident again.

Ten seconds later, I asked, "What happened?"

At that moment, Jeannie realized that I had short-term memory loss. As this question-answer-forget-question cycle continued, she was terrified that I would not remember the life that we were planning to create together. Meanwhile, as a steady stream of my fellow residents visited, I recognized them.

"Hey, Doug," I said. "What's up? What happened?"

"You had a cardiac arrest while playing in the basketball game," Doug said. "The anesthesiologists resuscitated you. You had to be shocked and tubed. Now you're at Harborview Hospital MICU recovering."

"Oh," I said, as if hearing this for the first time.

Doug walked away from the bedside for a minute, then returned.

"Hey, Doug!" I exclaimed, happy to see him. "What happened to me?"

This cycle replayed all evening with each visitor. My fellow residents must have been thinking, *What a tragedy. How will he be able to finish his training? I wonder if he knows he's been planning his wedding, and is due to be married in five months? Wait a minute! SHIT, I'm going to have to take his Emergency Room call!*

The elephant in the room loomed large, as everyone feared the worst: *Would Herman go from being a well-educated orthopedic surgeon-in-training to a babbling idiot right before our eyes?*

No one was more afraid of that than Jeannie. As she contemplated our future, she stayed with me for the first two nights, sleeping in a reclining chair.

Meanwhile, in Los Angeles, my father also feared the worst. He had left L.A. at 7:00 in the morning to make the nearly 700-mile, 18-hour drive up the Interstate 5 corridor through California, Oregon, and Washington. He'd intermittently call my mom to say, "I'm still going, and I'm going to go a little further."

"Don't drive the whole way without stopping," Mom insisted. "Please stop along the way."

He never stopped until he reached the University of Washington Medical Center ICU, one of the country's best hospitals at the time, where I had been transferred. When Dad pulled up at the hospital, Jeannie greeted him at his car.

"Hi Dad, you're here," she said, thinking, *He looks like he's been through hell -- and he has, emotionally.* The inside of the car looked like a tornado had torn through it. About 30 empty Coca-Cola cans and bottles, as well as potato chip bags, were strewn on the passenger seat and floor. Clearly, he had been chugging Coke and snacking on chips to stay awake during the long drive.

Jeannie escorted him into the room, and my dad hugged me.

"Where's Mom?" I asked.

"Mom's home," he said. "She's coming later."

We chatted for a few minutes. Then I said, "Hi, Dad, you're here. Where's Mom?"

"Mom's home. She's coming later."

This happened over and over. A short time later, he called my mother, who was double-locked in the county inpatient psychiatric ward. She was alone in her office with the door closed. She is a very private person who did not share her personal affairs with her colleagues.

"Mom," my father said, his voice cracking with despair, "I just had to call you. I couldn't handle it anymore."

She interpreted his tone of voice to mean that I was dead. The thought of losing her only remaining child was unbearable; she screamed and pounded on the desk. Her colleagues on the ward, who knew her son was a doctor, immediately converged to comfort her. She had to tell them the bad news. Dad, of course, reassured her that I was alive, but her emotions raged until she calmed down.

Soon after being admitted to the University of Washington Hospital, doctors determined that I had Right Ventricular Dysplasia, a rare heart disease that causes fat to replace muscle. This condition triggers vulnerability to dangerous arrhythmias; antiarrhythmic medication was the only treatment at the time. Though genetic, I was the only person in my family with a heart problem.

Meanwhile, an optimistic, young cardiologist visited us to share what sounded like good news.

"There is an experimental treatment for the kind of heart disease that you have," he said. "It's a brand-new procedure. We implant a small pacemaker with the capability of a defibrillator into your chest. Every time your heart races into an irregular rhythm or stops altogether, the device will shock you to restore a normal heartbeat. The shock will save your life."

I envisioned the violent impact of defibrillator paddles jolting the human body with electricity. I had seen patients jerk upward too many times. The patient didn't feel it, because he or she was technically dead, but it was a horrific sight.

"Wouldn't it be extremely painful to get defibrillated while I'm conscious?" I asked anxiously.

The doctor shrugged. "Not really. It just feels like a real strong hiccup. Do you want to try it?"

"Sure," I said. "What do I have to lose?"

I would be on antiarrhythmic medication to control my heart rate, and the defibrillator would simply be a backup. Surgery was scheduled. Despite my relief and hope that this device could stabilize my body and keep me alive, an avalanche of bad news soon cast a dark cloud over me.

First, I developed aspiration pneumonia, triggered by vomiting and gagging on the breathing tube during that first day in the hospital. Stomach contents had lodged in my lungs, causing infection. Another infection was festering, caused by the extremely unsterile conditions of the gymnasium floor when my fellow residents had inserted a central line in my neck. Bacteria around the catheter tube had developed into line sepsis, a blood infection that can become life-threatening.

As this double-whammy ravaged my already-weakened body, the life-saving surgery was delayed by two weeks. All I could do was lie in bed, praying for a quick recovery and a successful procedure to implant the defibrillator.

Many people visited; some were upbeat and encouraging, but others wore sad expressions that mirrored and exacerbated my misery. Thankfully, Jeannie and my father were my constant companions, brightening the gloom of the hospital room and uplifting my spirit. At the same time, I received incredible care from doctors and nurses who went above and beyond. One nurse massaged me with warm lotion. Another nurse put me in a wheelchair with a heart monitor attached and treated me with excursions to the hospital patio.

Every time a nurse wheeled me back through the bustling ICU corridor, I smiled as we passed "the patient board," which listed the first and last names of every patient in the unit. Since I was a resident who was training at this hospital, my attending physician worried that the steady stream of visits from my fellow residents was depriving me of rest. To protect my privacy — this was, of course, back in the days before the existence of HIPPA and other privacy laws — my attending suggested using an alias for me on the patient board. What was my only choice for an alias? STEVEN SEAGAL, the actor and martial artist whom I admired. He epitomized mental and physical strength, as well as courage, and I desperately needed that.

Meanwhile, my mother finally secured a replacement at work and arrived in Seattle two weeks after my cardiac arrest.

"Mom!" I exclaimed as she hugged me. While horrified at my condition, she was grateful that I was alive. Her presence, along with my dad and Jeannie, provided tremendous comfort, as did the arrival of my brother Bill, who flew in from Boston. When Bill walked into the room and observed me lying on the bed, he looked scared. But I was thrilled to see him.

"My brother is wearing jeans!" I said in awe. "My brother never wears jeans!"

After hugs and light conversation, Bill switched into cardiologist mode, studying the monitor and my heart rhythm. He also went to the nurses' desk to check it. He was gone for two minutes before returning to my bedside.

"Oh, my God!" I exclaimed, as if seeing him for the first time. "My brother has on a pair of jeans!"

Bill sobbed, devastated by my short-term memory loss. However, tears of joy streamed down the faces of my parents and my fiancée. They were relieved that I was starting to remember some things — and that I would not be like this for the rest of my life.

CHAPTER FOUR

The Shocking Pain of My Dead Dream

WHILE WAITING FOR MY infections to resolve and remaining at risk for another cardiac arrest, I was monitored around the clock in my room in the ICU. Weak from the infections and subsequent weight loss, I was also recovering from soreness caused by the chest compressions and multiple defibrillations that had saved my life.

Now, my heart frequently and suddenly spiked into a rapid heart rate of 150 to 200 beats per minute. A normal heart rate is 50 to 80 beats per minute. These heart-racing episodes were terrifying. The only treatment, if my heart rhythm did not correct itself, was for the hospital staff to use an external defibrillator to shock my weak, aching body. Fortunately, these racing-heart spells stopped just as quickly as they began. One day, however, an excessively high heart rate started — and didn't stop. Fear of getting defibrillated made my heart race more out of control.

Fast footsteps echoed from the hallway as the code team ran toward my room with a crash cart. I could only lie there, dreading the pain if they resorted to shocking my heart back to a normal rhythm.

My cardiologist burst into the room first. The code team stood around him, waiting for him to bark his first order. But he simply stared at me with a strange and stern expression, as if he were contemplating something. Without warning or words, he balled his fist. With the force of a sledgehammer —

Thump!

He whacked the bottom of his fist straight onto my chest!

"Ow!" I groaned.

The crash team stared in stunned silence.

He said, "I've always wanted to do that."

The good news? His action stopped my accelerated heart rate.

Even though the wallop hurt terribly, I appreciated my doc's special brand of humor. He had just delivered a precordial thump. If this maneuver occurs at the onset of a racing heartbeat, it can actually stop the rapid beats. How? A strike to the chest can generate four to five joules of current and correct the heart's rhythm.

After that, as I continued to heal in preparation for surgery, the days were long and slow. I watched MTV, CNN, BET, and what became my favorite soap operas, *General Hospital* and *All My Children*. The shows provided quite a distraction, but not enough to prevent me from doing a lot of deep thinking. Overall, my thoughts were grim.

I remembered my high school report about Swiss psychiatrist Elisabeth Kübler-Ross and her 1969 book, *On Death and Dying*, which she wrote after working with gravely ill patients. How ironic that I was now thinking of her Five Stages of Grief in terms of my own life all these years later! I contemplated each Stage: denial, anger, bargaining, depression, and acceptance.

Was I in denial? Of course, part of me wanted to believe that I could make a full, miraculous recovery from this ordeal and step right back into my dream life. What about anger, bargaining, depression, and acceptance? I was an emotional roller coaster, riding the peaks and plunges of each emotion from moment to moment.

At long last, I was ready for the surgery to insert my defibrillator, making hospital history as the youngest person ever to undergo this procedure. During the surgery, a lateral thoracotomy cut was made between my ribs. This incision allowed for perfect exposure of my heart and for placement of the sensory patches around it. My heart rate would be constantly monitored, and the defibrillator would automatically be instructed on what treatment to initiate if an irregular heart rate developed.

At the same time, a Pacemaker Cardioverter Defibrillator (PCD) was inserted in my left abdomen above the muscle and below the skin, just above my waistline. I would eventually learn to get used to its prominent bulge that was approximately the size of a small, thick iPhone; it actually measured five-by-four-by-two inches. Wires attached to its main component — often called the "can" — which connected to the heart patches, and could detect a rapid heart rate, then signal the defibrillator to deliver the shock. A battery with a five-year lifespan powered the defibrillator.

This device, made by Medtronic, was still undergoing clinical trials, and was not yet approved by the FDA. The difference between a much smaller pacemaker and a defibrillator is that a pacemaker provides only one function: it constantly forces the heart to beat at a normal pace. On the other hand, my "smart" defibrillator had the ability to choose from several pacing and shock therapy protocols:

- A heart rate below 48 beats per minute would trigger the device to function as a pacemaker, commandeering the heart to beat at a rate higher than 48.

- For a rate between 48 and 160, no therapy was needed.

- For a heart rate between 160 and 180, the device would attempt to "capture" the rapid rate and pace me down below 160.

- For a heart rate over 180, the device would pace three times to lower my heart rate. If that failed, the device would deliver 15 joules of life-saving electric shock — then 30 joules, then 45 joules, within milliseconds, if necessary — to jolt my heart back into a normal rhythm and prevent possible deterioration to cardiac arrest.

I went into surgery weighing 160 pounds, and came out 20 pounds heavier. My body swelled like a water balloon, due to retention of fluids given intravenously during the procedure. Jeannie and I still laugh at how my scrotum looked like a small balloon that had to be propped up on a wash cloth so I could be comfortable. Thankfully, I deflated as my body slowly excreted all that fluid.

After surgery, I was relieved to have a defibrillator, but nervous about if or when it might go off. *Would it work? Would it hurt?* While the defibrillator was my lifeline — designed to serve as the last step to preventing a cardiac arrest — my primary mode of therapy was anti-arrhythmic medication, which slowed the heart rate. Unfortunately, only guidelines were provided for dosages. Each patient was unique, and my doc put me on the lowest possible dose: 25 milligrams of a beta blocker.

As I navigated my postoperative hospital stay that was supposed to last one week, I spent a lot of time in bed, forced to swallow several huge potassium "horse pills" that kept getting stuck in my throat.

Meanwhile, as if I hadn't endured enough, my throat became inflamed. This triggered a rip-roaring case of post-surgery esophagitis, which is inflammation of the esophagus, the tube that carries food from the throat to the stomach.

As a result, eating solid food was terribly painful. We struggled to find anything that I could eat. One day, our friend Ellen visited and suggested, "Jeannie, why don't you try feeding him baby food?"

Voilà! This worked. And when Jeannie advanced me from baby food to oatmeal, we celebrated a hopeful moment in my recovery. In time, my throat finally mended, and I advanced to eating solid foods.

But after nearly three weeks in the hospital, my morale was extremely low. *How long will I be in this medical prison?* Excruciating pain and muscle spasms at the incision site kept me grimacing all day and night. My requests for more painkiller roused suspicion from one unsympathetic nurse, who was convinced that I just wanted more narcotics for the high. Apparently, the typical defibrillator patients — who were 30 to 40 years older than me — did not complain of this much pain because their muscles had atrophied and therefore caused less discomfort from muscle spasms.

At last, my surgeon confirmed my legitimate need for pain medication, but one cruel nurse disregarded the doctor's order to administer it intravenously. She said if I wanted it, she would only give it intramuscularly, thinking that if I really didn't need it, I wouldn't want to be stabbed in the muscle. Of course, I did need it. I took it like a man, despite the intense pain when she injected an intra-muscular needle into my thigh, which was now skin-and-bone.

One day, reality smacked me in the face. I discovered that I looked just as bad as I felt. This happened after I managed to get out of bed and look in the mirror. My formerly muscular chest was totally flat. I had swelled from a normal weight of 160 pounds to a postoperative weight of 180, then withered down to 135 pounds. I looked like a different person.

Despite this dramatic outward change, my bride-to-be loved me in sickness and in health. Sadly, a few people questioned her devotion by asking, "Jeannie, are you still going to marry Herman?"

"Yes," she answered without hesitation. She never considered leaving me or canceling the wedding. Instead, she focused on getting me healthy and back on my feet so we could enjoy the rest of our lives together. Yet Jeannie did wonder whether I could recover in time for our wedding that was scheduled for September 7, 1991.

Her unwavering devotion to my recovery inspired her to quit her job to stay at my bedside all day. I hated to imagine the loneliness, fear, and fatigue that Jeannie must have felt, leaving her fiancé in the hospital at night, then coming home to do homework. Once my Dad arrived, they walked to the car together every evening.

For me, time seemed to stand still. Day after day, I stared outside as the relentless Seattle rain streamed down the window of my hospital room. *Am I ever going to get out of here? What am I gonna do? All my dreams have been blown up! Not side tracked. Blown up!*

I begged God to help me understand what was going on, and why. Believing in something greater than myself was comforting, but I was baffled about why I had seemingly made all the right moves to embark on a noble career, only to experience what felt like punishment.

At the same time, I accepted that suffering is a relative experience. Yes, I was sickly and confined to a hospital bed with an uncertain future. *But I was alive!* My deep faith left no doubt that God had spared my life, and for that, I was extremely grateful. He had enabled me to dramatically beat the odds. At the same time, my work in hospitals prior to this crisis had taught me that one person's suffering could be enviable by someone who was enduring a worse fate, and that resilience always trumps pain. During infrequent flashes of optimism, I clung to hope that God had a greater plan for my life than I could ever conceive for myself. I just had no idea what that could be.

On May 28, 1991, four weeks after my premature death, my doctors let me go home. I had been in bed so long, I couldn't even walk out of the hospital. Jeannie pushed me in a wheelchair — the kind with the thin, five-foot pole that prevented patients from stealing the chairs — down the long, familiar hallways where I had seen my patients for the last three years. What a melancholy moment to think about how the roles had changed! My somber reality only worsened after Jeannie and my father got me into the car.

The ride home was excruciating. I cried out in pain as my father drove too fast, hitting every pothole and bump along the way. The car jostled my body, which aggravated my fresh surgery wound. It was unbearable, and I groaned, "Oh, oh, oh, Daddy, Daddy!" Thankfully, Jeannie later became the designated driver, since she was familiar with the streets and avoided the potholes, sparing me from extra pain.

At home in our two-bedroom condo, attempting to lie in bed was an exercise in sheer agony. The movement tugged on the smiley-face-shaped incision that started four inches below my left armpit, came forward seven inches between ribs five and six, and ended just below my left nipple.

Each time I attempted to lie down in the least painful way, I envisioned my anatomy instructor, who always wore a bow-tie and long white coat signifying his rank. As I grimaced and slowly adjusted my body, I could still hear him saying, "It takes at least six muscles to position yourself flat. The rectus abdominis is the main muscle, starting at the pelvis and connecting to the fifth, sixth, and seventh ribs. Other muscles — such as the iliopsoas, tensor fasciae latte, rectus femoris, sartorius, and obliques — are also recruited to assist the rectus abdominis."

My anatomical understanding of my physical plight did nothing to help me lie flat. And because I could tolerate a seated position, we purchased a lovely (albeit poopy-brown-colored) corduroy La-Z-Boy. We kept it in the living room, and I slept in it, while Dad dozed in the spare room, and Jeannie rested in our bed.

Settling in at home did not alleviate the fear, anxiety, and onslaught of questions consuming me. *When would the experimental device in my chest fire? Would it hurt? Would the medication work correctly, so my heart rate would never become abnormal enough to trigger the defibrillator to shock me? Was I receiving the correct dosage of heart medicine? What if I exerted myself and my heart rate increased? Would I get shocked while Jeannie and I were intimate? Had Jeannie's round-the-clock care of me for the past month left her exhausted and burned out?*

She needed a break, but did not want to leave me to attend her best friend's wedding in New Hampshire. She had committed to serve as a bridesmaid long before our lives changed so drastically. My father and I convinced her to go, reassuring her that my memory was steadily improving, and that I would be fine at home with him. We were wrong. Her absence plunged me into another phase of short-term memory loss. I could, ironically, remember incidents from 20 years earlier, but things that happened 20 minutes ago were fuzzy or downright blank. At one point, I looked at my incision in the mirror and asked, "Dad, what happened? Where's Jeannie?"

He answered, "You had a cardiac arrest and had to have surgery to put in a device to control your heart rate. Jeannie is in New Hampshire."

It felt like forever that she was gone. I asked, over and over, "What happened? Where's Jeannie?"

At first, my father patiently answered. But after a while, he became so frustrated that he wrote JEANNIE IS IN NEW HAMPSHIRE on index cards and set them on the breakfast table in front of me.

Despite my memory troubles, I was slowly regaining strength, and exercised by walking to the mailbox through our building's extremely long hallway.

This hallway is like a scene in the freaking Twilight Zone, I thought. As I took seemingly endless steps to reach the mailbox, the hallway seemed to get longer and longer. One day I took the mail back to our condo, sat down, and looked at the name on the front of an envelope: "Herman Williams, MD."

"Oh, crap!" I exclaimed. "Dad, I'm a doctor! I'm a doctor!" I had forgotten that I was a physician! Though devastated, I burst out laughing. "I'm a doctor, dammit! Daddy, I'm a doctor."

Next came a white doctor's coat embroidered with my name: Herman Williams, MD. It also said *Chief Resident* because I was slated to become one of the chief residents. My dad hung the white coat on the closet door to help me remember that I was a doctor.

Unfortunately, even with the index card reminder, I continued to ask, "Daddy, where's Jeannie?"

"I can't take it anymore!" my father cried. "You've got to remember what happened!"

Watching my dad break down was awful. He was probably thinking he would have to take care of me for the rest of his life. The horror of witnessing his pain literally jump-started my short-term memory. From then on, I remembered that Jeannie was in New Hampshire.

She returned, and Dad stayed with us until my post-operative course stabilized in July. His departure after a long stay with us inspired me to reflect on my father's constant devotion throughout my life: always supporting me, at every football game, track meet, piano recital, and graduation, and always serving as my mentor and cheerleader. My father's immense love and dedication overwhelmed me with gratitude.

I was also grateful and excited that Bill was scheduled to visit again. One day before his arrival, Jeannie and I were complying with the Catholic Church's requirement for pre-marital counseling. We were rushing around the condo, trying not to be late. I was sitting on the edge of the bed, when suddenly my heart started racing.

Bam!

A slap sound resonated from my chest, which simultaneously felt slammed by a hammer. I swore as loud as I could, holding my chest.

"Oh, my God, what just happened? Jeannie, I think I just got my first shock."

"What did it feel like?"

"Like a horse kicked me from inside my body," I said. "And the only warning was sudden, rapid heart rate. Now it's back to normal."

Jeannie was horrified as she sat beside me. Her expression was a combination of wide-eyed anxiety and fear along with the steady, objective analysis of a nurse trying to assess her patient's condition. I was afraid to move, not knowing if sudden movement would trigger another heart rate increase. At that point, we realized that my doctor had provided no instructions on what to do if I got shocked, except that I had to go to the hospital if I got zapped multiple times.

"I'll call the doctor," Jeannie said.

"Call Bill," I said as terror gripped me. *Was I on the verge of another cardiac arrest? If so, would the defibrillator do its job and save my life? I* felt a twinge of anger that the doctor had told me a shock would feel like a "strong hiccup." The truth was: it hurt like hell!

Bill arrived the next day. As a cardiologist, he was fascinated by my survival story and every detail of my treatment and recovery. In fact, he became a consultant on my medical care, demanding to know everything about my medications and device. His caring concern, coupled with his brilliant medical expertise, were tremendously comforting for both Jeannie and me. One day, as Bill escorted me down the long condo building hallway to the mailbox —

Bam!

I swore at the top of my lungs, grasping my chest, reeling from the pain of a horse-kick to my heart. I wanted to cry.

Bill's face lit up. He burst out laughing.

"Herman, it works! It works!"

"Oh, crap!" I yelled. "It hurts! It hurts!"

"Herman, it works!" Bill doubled over with laughter, which he cannot stifle even today when he recalls that awful moment. Why? Because he had learned about defibrillators in theory, but had never seen one working in real life. So, watching it work, while saving his brother's life, filled him with joy. I felt no such elation as he escorted me back to my room. I laid down, depressed and horrified that I could have just dropped dead.

This incident taught me that rushing was a trigger for a shock. Being late for an appointment or hurrying to get out of the house, for example, created the highest probability for getting zapped. Jeannie and I also learned that a single shock simply required us to notify the doctor on call. And if I got jolted multiple times, I had to go to the hospital so doctors could determine the cause and resolve it.

Meanwhile, at my parents' insistence, we purchased a home with an extra bedroom, in case they needed to come and take care of me. Our friends packed up our condo, and we moved.

As I continued to gain strength, our wedding day arrived. On September 7, 1991, Jeannie and I were married in St. Cecilia Church in Boston, Massachusetts. Jeannie was there physically, but mentally, her mind whirled with scenarios of me getting defibrillated in front of a church full of people. She was totally distracted, thinking about a plan to get me out of there.

At one point, she turned around and everyone, even the priest, was teary-eyed. But not Jeannie; we laugh today when she says, "I wasn't crying because I didn't want to ruin my make-up and the wedding pictures." Thankfully, we got through the wedding and everything was fine.

After that, we flew to the Caribbean island of St. Maarten for our honeymoon. Jeannie and I were nervous that I might get shocked, especially when we realized that it was reckless to leave the country five months after my cardiac arrest. My life was depending on an experimental device that the FDA had not even approved, and which was not even being used in any other country. Despite this risk, we enjoyed a wonderful, mostly shock-free honeymoon. On the last day, we checked out and were waiting by the pool for our ride to the airport.

Bam!

I swore out loud as the familiar horse-kick walloped my chest. Jeannie pulled me into a cabana and closed the curtains. We were terrified that I would get shocked during the ride to the airport and the long wait for our flight. Back home, because I'd had three shocks in five months, my doctor increased my medication dosage to control the arrhythmias.

A few weeks later, my parents hosted a wedding reception in Los Angeles for our family members. Then Jeannie and I held a third reception with our friends in Seattle. The event was lovely, and provided an opportunity for me to speak to the 30 people — including Jeannie, my parents, Bill, aunts, doctors, and nurses — who were beaming with love and compassion. When I rose to make a speech, emotions jolted through me, my eyes filled with tears, and I began in a quavering my voice:

"I just want to express my immense gratitude to all our friends, relatives, and medical staff who helped me survive my cardiac arrest. And I couldn't have made it without —"

Bam!

Oh, crap! I got shocked for the first time in front of a crowd. Perhaps they thought I was playing. Jeannie and Bill knew I was dead serious, and they walked me to the stairs near the door to the garage.

Bam!

Zapped again. I sat down. This was the first time I was shocked more than once. We decided to go to the ER. I tried to get up.

Bam!

Jeannie pressed on to get me to the car, and I got jolted one more time.

"This is wonderful!" Bill exclaimed. "Herman, it's saving your life!"

Unamused and unimpressed, Jeannie and I glared at him like, *Are you crazy?*

I just wanted to die! How could I live like this? It was like some Pavlovian experiment. Every time my heart sped up, I was crippled by fear, wondering if I would get a shock. The stimulus was so horrific to get 30 to 45 joules of current delivered internally, while helplessly awake to enjoy the fun.

My father took the wheel. I endured the ride from hell as he sped over what seemed like every pothole in Seattle, jostling my body and aggravating my incision. Exacerbating that physical pain were five more horse kicks hammering my chest, for a total of seven shocks before we arrived at the Emergency Department.

After that, I was told that five months of trauma to my mind and body had earned me a clinical diagnosis of Post-Traumatic Stress Disorder (PTSD). I became terrified of being shocked in public, and was therefore increasingly fearful of leaving the house. Then I began having "Phantom Shocks"[1-2]— waking up in a cold sweat, believing that I'd been defibrillated, even though the device showed no shock had been given. This inspired me to see a therapist for PTSD and mild depression.

In November, seven months after my defibrillator was implanted, a physician who heard about my situation approached me and asked if I was interested in using hypnosis to recount my subconscious thoughts and feelings prior to the arrest. Jeannie and I believed this might help alleviate the depression, so I agreed. The session started out fine; Jeannie was in the room with us.

The doctor began with a soothing tone, "Herman, close your eyes and take deep breaths. Go back to the day of the cardiac arrest. Now count backwards from 10."

I counted slowly, "Ten, nine, eight, seven, six, five, four —"

My heart suddenly began to race.

---

1   Swygman CA, Link MS, Cliff DL, et al. *Incidence of phantom shocks in patients with implantable cardioverter defibrillators. Paper presented at: Annual Meeting of the North American Society of Pacing and Electrophysiology; May 6—9, 1998; San Diego, Calif.*

2   Kowey PR, Marinchak R, Rials S. More things that go bang in the night [letter]. *N Engl J Med.* 1993;328:1570—1571

Bam! I got shocked.

Bam! A second jolt.

Bam! A third.

Each jolt made me yell in pain. Then this quack doctor freaked out. He tried to inject a syringe of Valium directly into my vein.

"Call 911!!!" Jeannie shouted.

Bam! Four.

Bam! Five.

Bam! Six.

I yelled in pain with every zap. And with each shock, my heart slowed down, then sped up again, over and over. The paramedics eventually arrived and raced me to the hospital. En route, I was shocked repeatedly.

Every defibrillation intensified my panic into what I call "the circle of fear:" my heart races, triggering anxiety about getting a jolt; the defibrillator fires, making me even more anxious; my heart races faster, sparking another shock; my heart rate accelerates even more rapidly. The higher my heart rate, the greater the likelihood that my defibrillator will zap me to calm my heart to a normal rhythm. It felt like a herd of wild horses was trampling through my chest as I was shocked 25 consecutive times, before reaching the emergency room.

God, just take me! I prayed.

I was crying, trembling, and unable to speak when we arrived at the ER. Doctors stopped this horrific episode by slowing my heart rate with five milligrams of Valium. However, my physicians' inability to find an effective, long-term medication to control the random defibrillations was the reason that shock episodes were tormenting me three to four times each month. As a result, I suffered debilitating anxiety that I could get zapped at any moment.

Would this terrifying limbo plague me the rest of my life? How long would I suffer with this condition? How could I actually live like this? Assuming I recovered, what kind of life would I have? Would I be able to work as a doctor? Would I realize even a fraction of my dream of being an orthopedic surgeon in Los Angeles?

Another distressing experience occurred when I forgot to take my medication. My racing heart woke me at 3:00 a.m. Fear gripped me as I lay on my stomach, eyes wide open in the darkness.

Bam!

The shock was so intense and so painful that my body went airborne. I flipped like a pancake, landing on my back, stunned. Of course, my obscene shouting and *Exorcist*-like movement awoke Jeannie. She turned on a lamp, which illuminated beads of sweat on my forehead. I swore out loud as I got popped one more time. Jeannie got me downstairs into the car for the 15-minute drive to the hospital.

"Jeannie, you're so strong," I said as she sped through red lights on deserted streets.

"No, honey," she said with a trembling voice. "Inside I'm dying. I'm so scared; everything inside me is emulsifying, like the fear is going to ooze out of me."

The angst on Jeannie's face mirrored mine; being a newlywed was supposed to be a romantic adventure, not a series of terrifying health crises.

"Herman, when you hurt, I hurt," she said. "The nurse inside me always kicks into autopilot. I switch from wife to caretaker, and get you to the hospital. Maybe I left nursing school because the universe knew that you would be my lifelong patient. I'm grateful I can be that for you."

From the start and to this day, I have been overwhelmed with gratitude toward Jeannie for lavishing me with genuine love while utilizing her clinical skills. Could I have been any more fortunate to have chosen a life partner who would, unbeknownst before my premature visit from the Grim Reaper, take such exquisite care of me — not out of wifely duty, but because she *wanted* to?

Here I was, this frail, 135-pound guy who was getting shocked all the time. I was an emotional wreck; being dependent on my wife for everything was difficult. My doctors forbade me from driving until I was shock-free for six months, which meant Jeannie had to take me everywhere. Many days, she took me to cardiac rehabilitation at 6:00 a.m. before attending classes during the day.

Her caretaker role dramatically changed our relationship; in the beginning, I was the outgoing extrovert, and she was very introverted. Then the roles switched. And that laid the foundation for our commitment to each other. We laughed together and cried together. Whenever I needed her, Jeannie was there. When I developed a rapid heart rate, she was the only person who knew how to comfort me. She was aware that I didn't like to be touched because it interfered with my ability to concentrate on my heart rate. Instead, she stood in front of me like my life coach and slowly coaxed me to calm down.

Without question, Jeannie's unwavering devotion empowered me to heal and triumph over the trauma of illness and my device. She could have left at any moment through it all, and anybody would have understood. At times, the stress was unbearable. But we hung in there and prayed that one day we would look back on these times and say, "Our love for each other saved us."

She was also supportive and comforting during the six months after my death, when the shocks made me afraid to leave the house. *What if I got zapped in the grocery store, or at the shopping mall, or in a restaurant?*

Despite this fear, I did muster the courage to return to my residency in early 1992. During that time, I loved to visit my patients to check on their progress and offer comforting words of encouragement. One patient in particular was a boy who was bravely battling terminal cancer. Back in 1990 before my own health crisis, I had treated 14-year-old John for osteosarcoma, the worst bone tumor possible, which required a leg amputation.

During his treatment, John's sweet face and spirit personified the heart-wrenching yet fulfilling nature of being a physician. My experience with John and his family also epitomized "the dream." It affirmed that I was a compassionate physician, with a great bedside manner. I loved my patients and treated them with respect; these qualities created a strong bond between me, John, and his family before he went home. Meanwhile, I felt fulfilled by helping and comforting people during their most devastating time of need. Sadly, two months after my cardiac arrest, John's cancer worsened, and his mother contacted me.

"Dr. Williams," she said. "I just wanted you to know that John heard about your cardiac arrest, and since he was getting much worse, he asked if he could donate his heart to you."

Her words and John's purity of spirit moved me to tears. Of course, John didn't know that we would both need compatibility testing and that you can't simply designate the person who might receive your heart. But his kindheartedness was the most incredible gesture that anyone has bestowed on me. When his death was imminent, I visited John in his hospital room. Joined by his parents and siblings, their pastor, as well as doctors and nurses, John asked us to say the Lord's Prayer with him.

"I love you all," he said, then exclaimed, "I see my grandmother!

She is there…in the light!"

"Go to the light," his family members said.

He stretched up his hands and breathed his last breath. That was one of the most beautiful moments I have ever witnessed. John faced death with absolute dignity, grace, and faith. At a time when most teenagers were enjoying high school and planning for college, his life was ending before it had even begun. I prayed for the strength to deal with my own challenges by emulating John's peaceful acceptance of this cruel wild card that life had dealt him.

As I attempted to resume my duties as a resident, it soon became apparent that my dream of being a surgeon had flat-lined along with my heart on April 28, 1991. Why? During operations, surgeons were required to use an electrical Bovie, an instrument that applies high frequency energy to cauterize the patient's blood vessels. My doctor and the manufacturer (Medtronic) of my Pacemaker Cardioverter Defibrillator (PCD) worried that the Bovie could create a magnetic field that might set off my defibrillator, causing an inappropriate shock. Any risk of jeopardizing my patient's safety — if I were defibrillated while performing surgery — was not an option. And because my doctors were still struggling to control my defibrillations with the right medication, I had to face the devastating reality that my dream of becoming an orthopedic surgeon was dead.

That ripped open a black hole inside me that was sucking me into a deep, dark depression. It forced me to reflect on the meaning of life and death. *Who I am? Why am I here?* If I could not execute the first life mission that I had chosen, what would I do now? My dilemma reminded me of a famous quote by Langston Hughes: "Hold fast to dreams, for if dreams die, life is a broken-winged bird that cannot fly." My wings were definitely clipped.

I found myself facing the edge of a cliff where I would plunge into an abysmal future that was bleak and blank. So, all I could do was look back... back into my past for answers.

CHAPTER FIVE

Death Inspires A Look Back At My Life

I AM JUST AN "average Joe" (Joseph is actually my middle name) born to loving African American parents who kept me on the straight and narrow, at least most of the time.

Gabrielle Beatrice Williams and Herman Johnny Williams welcomed me into the world to join them and my four-year-old sister, Janet. We grew up in a comfortable home in View Park, a middle-class neighborhood adjacent to Baldwin Hills in Los Angeles. We belonged to a local Catholic church, where Janet and I completed Catechism classes and Confirmation.

Both of our parents were psychiatric social workers for the Los Angeles County Department of Mental Health. Educated, socially conscious, and committed to helping people, they lavished us with love and instilled their mantra in us: "Janet and Herman Joseph, you can do anything you want to do."

My sister was brilliant and gifted with a beautiful singing voice. While I was also blessed with musical talent, neither she nor I applied ourselves academically. In fact, I was getting C's in elementary school and junior high school. All the while, teachers consistently told my mother that I had the ability to do well in school, if I applied myself.

I did — in music. To this day, my mother is extremely proud that I am a classically trained pianist. In fact, Emerson Junior High School made me the first student featured on their annual album. I played Beethoven's *Moonlight Sonata* at the junior high school concert. I found it absolutely enchanting to create beautiful music by allowing my fingertips to dance across the keys. The fact that other people could enjoy my performance made the experience indescribably wonderful.

Meanwhile, every day after school, Janet and I went to the clinic where Mom worked, and remained there until our father picked us up and took us home. I became fascinated by our parents' mission to help people who were sick from psychological problems. This fascination evolved to include the entire human body — and inspired me to identify medicine as a career aspiration. Yet my mother recalls how early on, I was somewhat fickle about my future career. Every time I had "Show and Tell" at school, I wanted to be whatever was "shown" that day.

"I want to be a sheriff," I declared after one such presentation.

My father responded, "Well, I thought you wanted to be a doctor."

"Oh yes," I said. "I'll be a sheriff in the summer and a doctor in the wintertime."

My shifting interests and lack of academic assertion made my mother question whether I was academically capable of becoming a doctor. Thankfully, in high school, I realized on my own that if I intended to leave my mark on this world, I needed to work diligently to raise my grades, set goals, and have the discipline to meet them.

Setting a higher standard for myself was my life's first major life challenge, and I worked hard to meet it. To my surprise, my grade point average soared to a 3.8, and I made the dean's list and honor roll in tenth grade at Beverly Hills High School. This aggressive pursuit of excellence and achievement laid the foundation for my future as a concert pianist and pre-med student.

My father often said with a proud glint in his eyes, "You are a Renaissance Man. That means being a man who is multi-dimensional and balanced with music, sports, church, academics, and a good social life. A true Renaissance Man can be and do anything he desires, and make a positive impact on himself, his family, and the world."

Unfortunately, as an industrious and ambitious Renaissance Man in the making, I encountered the sting of racism from an English teacher who was Caucasian. It happened after I wrote a paper based on a book and philosophy that my parents and their friends often discussed in our home: *On Death and Dying* by Dr. Elisabeth Kübler-Ross. In this epic book that's still relevant nearly 50 years after its initial publication, Dr. Kübler-Ross discusses the Five Stages of Grief.

When my teacher handed back my paper, she said in an accusatory tone, "You didn't write this paper. This is too good for you to have written." What she was really saying was that she believed it was too good for a black high school kid who couldn't possibly be that gifted at writing.

I defended the authenticity and originality of my paper and writing skills, and the discussion continued when my parents joined me and the teacher for parent-teacher conferences. It was always my policy that I participate in meetings and conferences involving my parents and teachers. Since they were going to talk about me, I felt strongly that I should be present. I also would not allow my mother to handle any problems I may have had at school.

"Mom, I'll take care of it," I always said. And I always did, adhering to a policy of complete honesty with my parents at all times.

As I excelled academically, I also played football and ran track. I met my best friend, Phil Morris, who's a year younger than me. Phil called me "Woody" — my nickname resulting from "riding the pine" during football games, meaning I sat on the wooden bench as opposed to playing.

"He never played football, but we both excelled in track and field," Phil recalls. "I was the captain and Herman was one of the most talented runners we had. He helped us win the league championship, and that's when we became friends. I was a high jumper, and Herman was a quarter miler and dominated the 440-yard competition."

Phil and I were part of a big, crazy social group comprised of athletes, performers, and guys who were doing not much of anything. Phil, whose father was actor Greg Morris of *Mission Impossible* fame, says, "At the young age of 17, I knew I'd be an actor. Herman was set on becoming a doctor. We shared ambition to be better people, and we needed to do something in our lives independent of our parents and friends. We're kindred spirits in that way. So, we began to travel different paths with the same motor and the same gas. That's refreshing to find in someone else."

When it was time to apply for college, my parents assumed I would attend the University of Southern California in Los Angeles, where my dad was an alumnus. At the same time, my girlfriend's mother, who was a guidance counselor at another high school, prompted me to apply to summer school back East. As a result, my girlfriend and I attended summer school at Phillips Academy in Andover, Massachusetts. I fell in love with New England and wanted to attend college there.

"Are you out of your mind?" my mother demanded when she and my father saw the cost of East Coast colleges. "How do you think we're going to pay for that?"

Meanwhile, despite my high school counselor's discouragement,

I was interviewing with recruiters from Dartmouth College, Harvard University, University of Pennsylvania, and Amherst College. Ultimately, I was graciously rewarded with an acceptance to one of America's most prestigious academic institutions: Amherst College in Massachusetts. This was an important brick in the foundation for my future as my dad's vision of me as a Renaissance Man.

However, my studies at this private liberal arts college were quite tumultuous. As one of only a few African American male students in my class, I often felt criticized and downright ostracized by blatant racism. I spent an inordinate amount of time defending my right to be enrolled in a traditionally white male college while simultaneously celebrating my African American heritage. Racial activism consumed me with heated discussions and verbal fights that were instigated by some white students' claim that an orientation for students of color would give us an unfair academic advantage. I also joined student sit-ins that occupied campus buildings. Similar events were occurring on campuses across the country, and they often made the national evening news.

I remember calling my father one night to warn him: "Dad, I want you to know that I'm with a group of students, and we're getting ready to take over the radio station and close it down. I just want you to know because: one, I could get arrested; and two, I could get kicked out of school."

The phone line was silent. My father finally asked, "Is it that important to you?"

"Yes."

"You realize you might have to come home?"

"Yes."

He replied, "Well, you do what you need to do."

At the last minute, our student group decided against committing a federal crime against the Federal Communications Commission by shutting down the radio station. We concluded that it would be more powerful to take over the administrative offices and strategize to shut them down.

We also held protests at the historic Charles Drew Memorial Cultural House, named for Dr. Charles R. Drew, a 1926 Amherst graduate whose research on blood transfusions and blood storage saved thousands of Allied soldiers' lives during World War II. Dr. Drew, who was African American, also challenged the American Red Cross' policy of racially based blood donations.

The night before the "take-over" of the school's administrative building, I became terribly ill with the measles and was admitted to a local hospital. Ironically, the measles spared me from the academic catastrophe of potential expulsion because I could not participate in the protest. That awful, contagious illness was a blessing in disguise for me at a school whose unofficial mascot, Lord Jeffery Amherst, gave smallpox-infected blankets to Native Americans to kill them so he could steal their land. (In January of 2016, Amherst trustees voted to stop using the vicious colonial commander as the mascot for the diverse and progressive school and community).

Unfortunately, my racial activism usurped my focus on becoming a physician. This became my second major life challenge because it was the first time I was told I didn't belong somewhere. I retreated into my mind and slumped to an all-time academic low. I actually received my first "F" in college. Imagine paying that kind of money to get a failing grade!

In the midst of this, I was inspired by a speaker at the Drew House, which hosted many events and lectures. Dr. Donald Parks spoke about how Dr. Drew changed the course of World War II, even though racism during the 1920s had banned him from American medical schools, and he was forced to go to Montreal, Canada, to earn his Medical Doctorate at McGill University.

Dr. Parks, who lived in Philadelphia and traveled the world representing SmithKline pharmaceutical company, was also president of the Charles Drew Society, which was dedicated to highlighting Dr. Drew's achievements. His rousing speech stressed the importance of black students excelling in academics and professional pursuits. He struck me as someone who could help save me from myself, so I approached him after the lecture.

"Dr. Parks," I said, "I need some advice, some direction. I'm very intent on becoming a physician."

"I'd be happy to help," he said.

I explained that my racial activism was hindering my academic achievement.

"If you really want to go to medical school," Dr. Parks told me, "you have to put your beliefs and concerns aside and focus on your grades. I'm here to tell you it can be done. By the way, here are some biographies of other black folks who did it throughout American history."

Dr. Parks assigned me to work on a project that required researching African American physicians such as Rebecca Lee Crumpler, the first African American woman in the United States to earn a medical degree, and Daniel Hale Williams, who founded a hospital with an interracial staff and who was one of the first doctors in America to perform open-heart surgery. He also invited me to Philadelphia to meet medical students, whom he instructed to monitor my progress through telephone conversations. All the while, he was showing me how to set up a circle of mentorship in which he mentored me to become successful, then serve as a mentor for others.

Dr. Parks became my first mentor, and he guided me on what I needed to do to get into medical school. During our first meeting, he asked me to send him my college transcript, grades, and scores from the Medical College Admission Test (MCAT).

"Herman," Dr. Parks said. "You have a good personality and are very approachable. But you have low grade point averages, including in math and science, and you have low MCAT scores. Your numbers just don't merit anybody taking a second look at your credentials. Medical schools are looking at paper."

Dr. Parks' grim prognosis did not temper my cocky attitude about graduating with a 3.7 GPA from prestigious Amherst College in the spring of 1980 with a Bachelor of Arts in Psychology. I remained convinced that I would be a shoe-in for medical school. *Wrong!*

I was rejected by all 15 medical schools to which I applied. As a result, I graduated with a great deal of resentment that I had wasted so much time playing the militant role in response to racial ignorance. I was also angry that I had robbed myself of the opportunity to enjoy the college experience.

The next year, I made a second attempt at applying to medical school — all of which again rejected me. This was one of the worst experiences of my life. And it was the first time that I had failed to achieve a goal; this defeat became the third major challenge in my life.

Dr. Parks recommended that I attend a post-baccalaureate program and take a year to boost my science grades, as well as re-take the MCAT. Instead, I languished for two years, beginning the summer after graduation when I studied at the University of Illinois in Chicago. After that, I worked as a pharmaceutical sales rep in Santa

Barbara, California. During that time, I kept in touch with Dr. Parks, who visited me and my parents during a four-hour layover in Los Angeles while traveling to Japan.

Dr. Parks, now a professor of medicine at Temple University School of Medicine and who operates a family medical practice in Philadelphia, recalls that visit well. "I sat down with them and explained what Herman had to do to be considered by medical schools. At the time, I was on the admissions committees at Thomas Jefferson University and Temple University, and I interviewed students almost weekly. Herman's numbers were very poor."

I was grateful for Dr. Parks' concern and assistance, but my morale and attitude were so low, I was ready to give up on my dream of attending medical school. I also came across outwardly as unwilling to do the work to elevate myself to the caliber of a student who would earn admittance into medical school.

"Herman, this is ridiculous!" Dr. Parks chided. "Unless you're going to do the work so people can look at you as someone who is a viable candidate for medical school, you're wasting my time and the schools' time."

His words slapped me in the face with reality. I hated the feeling of failure, and clung to my dream of being a physician.

"Herman, get back in school," Dr. Parks encouraged. "Do the best you can. Try to knock it out of the park."

I buckled down to show that I had the aptitude to attend medical school. First, I needed to excel in a post-baccalaureate program, so I applied at Creighton University in Omaha, Nebraska. Getting into Creighton would be my last chance to repeat the courses that I had not taken seriously at Amherst. This was literally my ticket to get into medical school.

During an interview with the program director, I asked, "What are you looking for in the students who will be accepted into this competitive program?"

"We're looking for people with potential," he said.

"Potential?" I echoed. "Potential is my middle name. In fact, if another person tells me I have the potential to be a great physician, I think I'll scream."

We both laughed, and he gave me a chance to re-embark on my dream. Once enrolled in a post-baccalaureate program, I repeated my science courses, eventually raising my science grades to a scholarly level. My diligence paid off; I was accepted to four medical schools. I elected to attend Boston University School of Medicine. *I was on my way, dammit!* The vision was becoming more clear. My success made Dr. Parks extremely proud; we became closer because I was showing him and others that I could do the work.

My plan was to excel in medical school, then get accepted into an orthopedic surgery residency, specialize in sports medicine, and return to Los Angeles to work for the Kerlan-Jobe Orthopaedic Clinic with Clarence Shields, MD.

To make this dream a reality, I had to do something exceptional, above and beyond the typical medical school applicant. So, I took a year off from medical school and attended the Harvard School of Public Health, graduating with a concentration in Health Policy and Management. My pursuit of this degree was inspired by President Bill Clinton's quest to insure healthcare as a right for all Americans. Though his efforts failed, it roused in me a hunger for knowledge and expertise in the subject that I believed would enhance my ability to deliver excellent medical care in the future.

While on the Harvard campus one day in 1987, I was going up

a staircase as a man was descending. A feeling that I knew him overwhelmed me. We looked at each other like, "I know you," but we had never met before. He was also a student in the School of Public Health. William "Bill" Daley and I instantly clicked without saying a word.

Bill, who is now an Executive Director of Cardiology at Novartis Pharmaceuticals in New Jersey, says we are "brothers from another mother." Though we look nothing alike, our personalities are very similar. I lived with Bill, who is three years older, for a few years. People saw us as brothers, calling him Godfather and me Consiglieri. My parents even began to call Bill my brother.

Also, while at Harvard, I met another person who would play an important role in my life: Augustus A. White, III, MD, PhD. He was chairman for the department of orthopedics at Beth Israel Hospital in Boston. Dr. White was the first African American to serve as a chairman for a clinical department in the Harvard Medical System. I had heard he was one of the greatest black physicians, and that he was the first African American to attend the Stanford University School of Medicine, so I was in awe when we met.

"Along comes Herman Williams, a bright, young, intelligent, athletic brother who was ambitious and wanted to do things," recalls Dr. White, who is now the Ellen and Melvin Gordon Distinguished Professor of Medical Education, and a Professor of Orthopaedic Surgery at Harvard Medical School. "I have good intuition when it comes to recognizing good people. When I meet someone, I can recognize talent and ability. I admired Herman and thought, 'Well, let me be his friend and work with him and see where we can go. He's a good brother. He's going to do good things. He deserves whatever help I can offer.'"

Dr. White, who is former director of the Oliver Wendell Holmes

Society, adds, "I had the good fortune of world-class mentors, and I'm very grateful for that. So, I let it flow through me and shared it with Herman. He was very responsive and appreciative. I shared some of my friends with him, including the NBA star and coach, K.C. Jones of the Boston Celtics. Herman and K.C. eventually formed a great relationship as well."

Along with introductions, Dr. White — author of the definitive book on the biomechanics of the spine — granted me the invaluable opportunity to join his research project and help him complete it. We eventually published an article entitled, "Prevalence of Idiopathic Vertebral Sclerosis, Zoetermeer, Rotterdam, 1975-1978," in the December 1991 edition of *SPINE*, a prestigious peer-reviewed journal.

"I get to know people when I co-author a paper," Dr. White says. "Writing the paper is cementing a mentoring relationship. I thought, 'If I can help him and give him encouragement and reinforcement, then I felt he would be very productive.' Herman did his fair share of the work and made a contribution and deserved to be a co-author in the article."

This was a prestigious honor because it associated me with the unparalleled achievement and respect that Dr. White enjoyed in the field of orthopedic medicine. For these reasons, I was extremely grateful that Dr. White became a key mentor in my life. He agreed to write me a letter of recommendation.

During the process of applying for a residency in orthopedic surgery, I wrote to Clarence Shields, MD, who had previously granted me a medical school rotation that introduced me to the different kinds of sports medicine practiced at the Kerlan Clinic.

As I approached graduation from medical school, it was time to apply for internships in general surgery and residency programs in orthopedics. At that time in America, not many people were getting into orthopedics, especially not many black folk. Knowing this, some of my African American friends discouraged me from pursuing a seemingly impenetrable area of medicine. The general message was, "They don't let black people into orthopedics. Are you crazy?"

My brother Bill encouraged me to go for it: "You're going to do it. That's all there is to it. Forget all those other haters."

I felt good that my many academic and professional accomplishments would elevate me above the competition.

Throughout medical school, I had kept in touch with Dr. Parks, who was eager to help me secure a residency. He called his good friend — the Associate Dean of the University of Washington School of Medicine — on my behalf. Dr. Parks told the dean, "I want you to take a look at this guy's credentials. He wants to be an orthopedic surgeon."

At the same time, Dr. White wrote a letter of recommendation to the selection committee to choose me as a resident in what was then one of America's top five orthopedic surgery programs.

My confidence was unbounded as I enjoyed support from Dr. Parks, Dr. White, and Dr. Shields. They were like the all-stars of medicine! With their endorsements, I felt the world would regard me as a future version of them.

As a result, I was invited for an interview, and successfully "matched" in orthopedic surgery at the University of Washington in Seattle, becoming only the second African American to do so. Meanwhile, I was blessed with a General Surgical Internship at Beth Israel Hospital. All of this happened through "the match" — a program in which medical students select residencies and vice versa; selections are announced on the much-anticipated "match day." I am convinced that my relationships with Dr. White and Dr. Parks secured my residency.

This immense blessing placed one more block in the foundation of my dreams. Now that I was on my way, I embraced my dream with vigor — the life I had so meticulously planned for, struggled to attain, and thought about endlessly — was all laid out before me!

All I had to do was complete my residency program, apply for a fellowship with the Kerlan Clinic, and move back to L.A. to become a physician for professional athletes. That one-year fellowship would put me on the inside track, and I felt so close to achieving my dream career that I could taste it.

But during the application process for the Kerlan fellowship, I died. So did my dream. Now, less than a year after my cardiac arrest, here I was — living in fear, pain, and disappointment punctuated by a diagnosis of Post-Traumatic Stress Disorder.

My heart was still beating, but I felt dead inside.

CHAPTER SIX

Now What?

I FELT LIKE THE cruel hand of fate had flushed my dream down the toilet. At 31 years old, I had been dreaming of becoming a doctor — and making all the right moves to do so — for more than half my life. Then, in one tragic heartbeat, it was gone.

This fourth major life challenge left me asking, *Why did this happen to me?* When no answers came, a dark cloud of depression consumed me.

My parents were unaware of just how sick I had become, until they visited me shortly after my favorite patient, John, died. We attended Sunday mass, and I became hysterical in church. After the priest took me somewhere to talk, my parents discovered that I rarely left the house, fearing a shock in public. Being mental health professionals, my mother and father were very worried about me.

I was showing classic signs of the Kübler-Ross Five Stages of Grief — specifically, anger and depression. I just couldn't understand how fate could so cruelly smack me down with this punishment when I was on the verge of receiving the rewards for all my hard work in academics and medical training. All day long, my gloomy brain churned with fear, sadness, and anxiety as I wondered, *Why, God, why?*

I felt it was impossible to enjoy life, or to acknowledge my many blessings. If Jeannie prepared a special dinner, it was difficult for me to savor and appreciate it, because my thoughts were consumed by grief over my dead dream and everything that I could no longer do or enjoy. I had been an athlete, with a muscular physique, physical stamina, and strength. All that was gone. I had no desire to play the piano. I wondered if my past passion for life would be forever dead along with my dream? The future looked bleak. My life as an orthopedic surgeon would have ensured an extremely comfortable life for myself, Jeannie, and the children that we hoped to have. But now, what would happen to my career? What kind of future did we have? Would we be able to have children? The weightiness of these questions, and my fear of the worst, crushed me into an even gloomier mood.

My depression began to ease when doctors finally found an effective medication. I enjoyed six months without a shock. Now allowed to drive, I found an alternate career, working as a counselor in the Office of Minority Affairs at the University of Washington. I also got involved with the School of Public Health. As I became less fearful of leaving the house or of being shocked in public, my PTSD symptoms began to subside.

I still consulted with Dr. Parks on occasion, who was very concerned that my health crisis would cost me the ability to sustain my well-being and livelihood. We talked about how I might transition as a physician into dermatology or radiology. Instead, I built on the Health Policy background I attained at Harvard by returning to school to earn a Master of Business Administration. Pursuing my MBA, would provide two years to stabilize my medication and build a new dream for myself.

All the while, my parents' mantra that they had repeated countless times during childhood echoed in my mind: "Herman Joseph, you can do anything you set your mind to." Their words bolstered my refusal to let fear or disappointment hold me down. This inspiration reflected on the major challenges I had overcome:

√ First, deciding to apply myself in high school;

√ Second, meeting the challenge of succeeding at Amherst College, despite the racial turmoil;

√ Third, embarking on a plan to earn scholarly grades and get into medical school;

√ And now, fighting to find meaning in life as I recovered from a major illness.

Mapping a new, uncharted future was just another personal challenge. My past successes convinced me that I would succeed once again. After being accepted into the University of Washington's Foster School of Business in the fall of 1992, I graduated in 1994 with a concentration in finance and a minor in healthcare.

All the while, Jeannie continued to support me while encouraging me not to give up. At the same time, she attended school to earn her bachelor's degree. She also graduated in June of 1994, and we bought a house in the Seattle suburb of Bothell.

I began working with the consulting firm, Arthur Andersen, as one of the first physicians to join the Pacific Northwest Healthcare practice. During that time, I had the privilege of meeting one of the most influential people of my life: Hugh Greeley, America's foremost expert in medical staff credentialing, quality, governance, and overall redesign relating to hospitals and medical staffs. We were introduced by a senior partner at Arthur Andersen, John Tiscornia, who invited me to a program at the Estes Park Institute, which provides seminars for hospital leaders.

Hugh vividly remembers how we met: "John said he wanted to introduce me to a young physician who was working on managed care issues with clients around Washington state. I had great respect for John, who said that Herman was a really quick, very bright, and delightful person. When John introduced us, that was my impression of Herman."

After our initial talk, Hugh invited me to join him on a client visit to a hospital system in San Jose, California. The objective was to help the two medical staffs merge into one. Hugh said it would be a good opportunity for me to observe how the politics and issues were resolved. I immediately said yes. During the two-day trip, Hugh encouraged me to participate in the meetings.

"Herman impressed me greatly through his studious silence, punctuated with either a very insightful question to the physicians at the table, or punctuated with a suggestion that allowed them to get over their political power fears," Hugh recalls. "Herman had a way of quite easily figuring out where people were and what they were thinking, then saying something to disarm them in a very polite, very gentle, but very meaningful way."

Also during that trip, we adopted Albert Einstein's saying: "All things should be as simple as possible, but not more so." Hugh says that I executed this tenet, for example, by completing a one-day job in a day, never taking longer than necessary.

After that, Hugh invited me to work on projects in other parts of the country, which I completed with great success. I had been completely unaware of this type of work until I met Hugh. He generously took me under his wing. We went on consulting engagements, just the two of us, for years. While I helped him build a consulting practice for The Greeley Company, he taught me everything I know about this field. Sometimes, even today, when I'm talking with hospitals, I say, "I'm a Hugh Greeley disciple."

The decision to embark in this new direction, with Hugh opening my eyes to new possibilities, was a godsend. It demonstrated that I was capable of excelling in a realm of healthcare that I had not targeted as a career interest or goal. Rather than dwell on what I wasn't doing as an orthopedic surgeon serving one patient at a time, I focused on how I was helping hundreds and thousands of patients receive better care by working with hospitals on policy and quality.

At the same time, my thinking began to shift into a more positive outlook. Rather than obsess about the big picture of my life, I savored the simple pleasures of being alive, married to a wonderful woman, and capable of earning a good living while meeting great new people and making a positive impact. Despite the constant undercurrent of anxiety that I could get shocked, and worries that my heart could give out before my fortieth or fiftieth birthday, I chose to think about the blessing of my second chance at life.

After all, I had *died* on April 28, 1991. My life could have all ended there. Period. That grim reality always shifted my thoughts to gratitude that *I'm still here!* And if I ever needed a reminder of my precarious health status, my heart always obliged.

Like the time in October of 1994 when I entered the men's restroom during a healthcare management retreat. In a stall, I pulled down my pants and took a seat. Suddenly without warning, I broke into a rapid and prolonged heart rate. The fear of getting shocked paralyzed me. All I could think was, *Pull up your pants slowly! They ain't gonna find me out cold in the bathroom with my pants around my ankles!*

I carefully inched up my pants.

"Call 911!" I yelled to a man who entered the bathroom.

I was rushed to the hospital. Thankfully, I did not get shocked. I was put on yet another new medication that had a lower side-effect profile. It had been two years since my last shock, but I kept having episodes of rapid heart rate. Since I had so many shocks in the past, this pesky heart rate issue wouldn't let me focus on moving on with life. I was put on another medication, which was effective for about a year.

Unfortunately, in early 1995, my worries turned to Jeannie's health. Spouses or significant others of folks who have a chronic illness frequently manifest the same symptoms, sometimes called "sympathy symptoms." Sure enough, Jeannie was having runs of a rapid heart rate. We were both paranoid that she might have some hidden heart disease as well, so we scheduled an appointment with the cardiologist at Northwest Hospital. While she was waiting to see the doctor, I went to the bathroom, where I started having palpitations. Before I could even unbutton my pants —

Bam!

One quick shock, out of the blue. However, my heart was beating so fast, I didn't feel it, because I nearly passed out. I was rushed into Jeannie's doctor's office and my defibrillator was interrogated. Imagine that, we came for Jeannie, and I stole the thunder. After a brief moment spent looking at a heart rhythm strip from my device, the doc said, "It appears that this new medication you were put on is not acting as an antiarrhythmic agent. It is, in fact, pro-arrhythmic for you."

Unbelievable! The medication was causing the abnormal rhythms! My doctor decided to simply back off the dosage and see if that made a difference. This approach seemed to work for several months, but I consistently had episodes of rapid heart rate, which always triggered fear of a shock.

In December of 1994, my doctor notified us that a new drug called Sotalol was specifically indicated for my Right Ventricular Dysplasia. We prayed that it would work for me. I was immediately hospitalized while doctors loaded me with Sotalol. It became instantly obvious that this drug also was pro-rhythmic and the trial was a failure.

We felt absolutely hopeless. We had tried so many drugs, and I was still getting shocked. The shocks were less frequent, but the defibrillator was supposed to be the backup, not the primary therapy. We needed a long-term solution. Consumed by despair, I was certain that I would die again, or be tormented by the pain and trauma of shocks.

In my gloom, I got this wild idea to try to conceive a child while in the hospital. So, we asked our friends to guard the door while we did the unthinkable in a hospital room! At the time, my thought was, *I might as well leave Jeannie someone to keep her company when I'm gone, someone to carry on the Williams name.*

More life-changing news evolved from that hospital stay: a drug called Cordarone was effective in other patients with my condition. My doctor hesitated to recommend it because its major side effect was a high probability of developing pulmonary fibrosis, which when taken for long periods, causes scar tissue in the lungs that interferes with breathing. I would essentially have to take it for my entire life, and being so young, the probability of pulmonary fibrosis was high. Since nothing else worked, Jeannie and I elected to try the drug.

In May of 1995, I was put on Cordarone. It worked! As the only drug that stabilized my heart rate, it changed my life. I was ultimately discharged on a low dosage of Cordarone.

Later that month, Jeannie blessed me with the news that she was pregnant with our son, Cole. Today I am still on Cordarone and have not developed pulmonary fibrosis. Praise God!

Putting the devastating challenge of erratic heart rates and the constant threat of shocks behind me, and looking forward to fatherhood, I stepped into what I call "the great years."

Enjoying time with my father, Herman Johnny Williams,
my sister, Janet Williams, and my mother, Gabrielle Williams.

With my first dog, Cleo.

In high school, I ran track and played football.

In high school, I participated in the Medical Explorers Club (left).
Also pictured is my graduation from Amherst College (right).

My parents.

Jeannie and I enjoying life before the cardiac arrest.

Jeannie and I celebrating on our wedding day.

Phil Morris with me.

Bill Daly with baby Cole.

We're always smiling when we're with our son, Cole.

Cole as a boy.

Cole's high school graduation.

My mentor,
Dr. Donald Parks.

My mentor,
Dr. Richard Allen
Williams.

My mentors have helped me excel academically and professionally.
They are: Hugh Greeley (top, left); Kent Wallace (bottom, left); and
Dr. Augustus White with me (right).

Featured on the cover of the 2015 edition InCharge Healthcare. From left: Edward Pearson, Hayley Hovious, Hon. William H. Frist, MD, Laura Beth Brown, and me. Reprinted with permission of Nashville Medical News.

CHAPTER SEVEN

The Great Years

"...And I will give you a new heart, and I will put a new spirit in you. I will take out your stony, stubborn heart and give you a tender, responsive heart."

Ezekiel 36:26

IT WAS FEBRUARY OF 1996 and the cold chill of the Pacific Northwest was in full effect. Jeannie and I were overjoyed with our one-month old son, Cole. While working at my first job out of business school, Arthur Andersen became unbearable. I felt like I was being abused and not appreciated.

"I'm going to resign," I told Hugh, who had become a close friend and mentor. "I can't take another day of this company. But I don't have another alternative."

"Go ahead and resign," Hugh said. "I'll make sure you have enough business, and I'll make sure you have a base salary."

Hugh sealed the transition to my entrepreneurial dream of having my own consulting firm. I will never forget the look on Jeannie's face when I told her that I was quitting my job when we had a one-month-old child. Despite the poor timing, she stood by me as always and encouraged me to do what I thought was best.

In March of 1996, I started a healthcare consulting company called Herman Williams Consulting. This business began from the ground up, providing clients across America with strategies to develop and re-organize hospitals, then offer a model to design the medical staff to best execute the hospital's mission. The company also helped hospitals with credentialing staff, updating bylaws, and following accreditation guidelines. I traveled a lot, and during the course of that hectic travel, I suffered one shock while running through an airport, fearing I would miss my flight. My doctor increased my Cordarone dosage, and all was well again.

In 1997, Hugh hired me as a full-time consultant as the Physician Medical Director in charge of The Greeley Company's external peer review program. Since this job was based in Marblehead, Massachusetts, outside Boston, Jeannie was thrilled when we moved to her hometown with Cole. Meanwhile, I thrived in my job, cherishing the rare opportunity of what I call my "Mini Hugh Greeley Fellowship."

Hugh taught me what he knew, and I ran with it, excelling in my external peer review work. I would find physicians in other parts of the country, perform external peer reviews for them, then produce a report evaluating their work as good or bad, while offering recommendations on how to improve. This work was really important to patient care. I was committed to always learning and improving, and Hugh facilitated my growth.

During this time, I enjoyed one glorious, peaceful year without a shock. This made it clear — I could live with a shock once every three to six years in exchange for a wonderful life, a great family, and a successful career. In the Five Stages of Grief, this constituted "bargaining."

And because anxiety could trigger a rapid heart rate and a subsequent shock, I let nothing faze me; I was cool as a cucumber.

"I've never seen Herman ruffled or angry," Hugh recalls, "so we loved to prank him. We had a friend who was good at mimicking voices, and we had him call Herman, pretending to be an irate CEO at the hospital where Herman had just completed a very difficult evaluation that resulted in a physician's summary suspension. Herman was as cool as he could be. He didn't get ruffled. Despite the angry caller's threats of legal action, Herman said something like, 'This is unusual. Don't worry, I'm sure it will work out fine.' It went on and on, and Herman's grace under fire came to light as he remained dignified and professional. Then we called him and said it was a joke. He always says he's going to get us back, and we still laugh about it today."

In 2000, Hugh paved the way for my transition from healthcare consulting to healthcare operations, enabling me to become a physician executive. It happened when one of my Greeley clients hired me as Vice President of Medical Affairs for CHRISTUS Health, overseeing three small hospitals in Beaumont, Texas.

I loved the work, and I was feeling so great that it was easy to almost forget that I was living with a heart condition. After all, it was now 2003 and I had been shock-free for seven years. However, one spring day, I was scheduled to give an audio conference for about 100 listeners across the country. I was anxious because I felt I had not prepared sufficiently and had been having a few runs of tachycardia intermittently throughout the day. As I sat at my desk in the administrative offices of St. Elizabeth Hospital in Beaumont, the runs resolved without incident. I grew more nervous as the call time approached. I felt like I was in a newsroom, as the conference call host announced, "OK, people, we are going live in 10 seconds!"

My heart beat faster. *Stay calm*, I repeated like a mantra in my head.

The announcer said, "OK, we're live in five, four, three, two, one—"
My pulse pounded as he continued, "Welcome to today's audio conference. Our guest speaker is Dr. Herman Williams."

"Hello," I said.

Bam!

I got shocked. I didn't know what to do, so I hung up immediately.

"Calm down," I said aloud. "Deep, slow breaths."

I checked my pulse, attempting to count the beats.

"Crap!" I couldn't count them, but my heart rate was fast.

Bam! Shock number two. *This is bad!*

I yelled down the hall for help. A colleague ran and called a "CODE BLUE" — hospital language for the team to respond to a cardiac arrest.

"Attention!" someone announced overhead. "This is the operator. We have a CODE BLUE in the administrative offices. I repeat, this is a CODE BLUE in the administrative offices."

Bam! Number three.

This plunged me into what I affectionately call the "circle of fear." Panic increased my heart rate, which triggered shocks, which caused a faster heart rate –– and more panic. Ultimately, the cardiac catheterization laboratory staff arrived in the administrative wing with a stretcher to take me to the cardiac catheterization lab where they would use special equipment to assess my heart.

"Dr. Williams," they said, "we need you to get on the stretcher so we can get you to the cath lab."

I froze with fear. Moving could speed my heart rate and trigger a shock, so I just sat there, holding my index finger to my heart, trying to count the beats. Because I was thin, I felt every beat through my ribs.

"DR. WILLIAMS!" a cath lab tech bellowed. "WE NEED YOU TO GET ON THE STRETCHER!"

I suddenly noticed who was speaking: an enviably handsome, muscular man who was about 6'2"and 180 pounds. His ripped chest and biceps were stretching the sleeves of his scrubs. All I could think was, *Damn, he's buff.*

He lunged toward me, wrapped his hands around my waist, and picked me up in one graceful movement, landing me gently and with perfect precision on the stretcher. It was a beautiful move. *Chinese judges? 10! U.S. judges? 10! Russian judges? 9.1! What? No perfect score.*

As we burst through the cath lab doors, my cardiologist barked, "Give him two milligrams of Valium and let's interrogate his device. Let's go, team!"

As the Valium coursed through my veins, the IV site burned. Warmth spread through my body. Finally, a normal sinus rhythm resumed. Unfortunately, my doc later delivered bad news: "You've developed a new and constant irregular heart rhythm."

Oddly, I felt at peace with my situation. I was grateful for the many years I had survived and thrived since the cardiac arrest. What did God have as the grand plan? How could a heart problem serve as the catalyst for helping me see what He was orchestrating for my life? Could I glean understanding from my cardiologist's new prognosis?

"Herman," my doctor continued, "the irregular heart rate is coming from one area in your heart. There's an ablation procedure that can only be performed by a select group of physicians in Boston. It's designed to actually burn out irregular tracts in the heart and potentially eliminate the arrhythmia."

Enter, major life challenge number five. It forced me to ask, *Should*

I agree to another experimental procedure, or was this the beginning of a cardiac decline?

I agreed to have the procedure. Besides, I had heard that Boston was nice in June and I was pretty sure a Sox game was coming up in the near future. Jeannie and I were nervous wrecks as we flew to Boston with Cole, who had just completed first grade.

"Oh, my God," she said, panicking on the airplane. "We're 35,000 feet in the air with no defibrillator. Oh God, please don't let anything happen."

We arrived without incident on Thursday for me to have pre-op blood work in preparation for the procedure on Monday. That Saturday, I was in the bathroom at Jeannie's parents' house when I spontaneously burst into a rapid heart rate. I waited for it to stop. No such luck.

"Jeannie, help me!" I yelled. My heart kept pounding vigorously. We ultimately made our way to the car outside. We sped toward the hospital. But a traffic jam at the Callahan Tunnel forced us to return to Jeannie's parents' house.

"Call 911," Jeannie told her sister as we remained parked in front of the house. To our surprise, two ambulances arrived, one right after the other.

The paramedics had to coax me into the ambulance, because I feared that any movement would trigger a shock. Two medics rode in my ambulance, while Jeannie traveled in the second ambulance. As our caravan approached the Ted Williams Tunnel, they parted the sea of cars, allowing us to speed to the emergency room at Beth Israel Deaconess Medical Center.

There, I told the EMT, "Fifty milligrams of IV Lidocaine has been known to slow me into a normal rhythm."

Since I was a physician, the EMT drew up 50 milligrams of Lidocaine and administered it stat, and I was hooked up to all kinds of beeping monitors.

Jeannie's sisters arrived shortly after us by car. She ran out to the lobby to make sure they were there. After they met, Jeannie ran back into the Emergency Department.

"Herman!" she shrieked. I was on the bed with my feet in the air, my body in the shape of the letter V. A grunting sound came from my open mouth. Jeannie froze in fear and shock.

The heart monitor was making a loud, steady sound — while the screen showed a flat line all the way across.

"Oh, my God!" Jeannie screamed. "He just died! My world just ended!"

She ran out of the room, and burst through the swinging doors so hard that they banged the walls. As she yelled for her sisters, a social worker escorted her into "the quiet room." Jeannie was sure that news of my death was imminent.

"Get Bill on the phone!" she shouted to her sisters.

Then the social worker explained that I was, indeed, alive. I'd had a grand mal seizure — apparently from the Lidocaine. While unconscious with violent muscle contractions, I had yanked the cords from the heart monitor, causing it to show a flat line.

Jeannie returned to the room. While relieved that I was alive, she was horrified by my condition. Doctors had ripped my jeans to inject anti-seizure medication into my thigh, which was now bruised. My cheek and tongue were swollen, because I had bitten them during the seizure. And I was bruised all over, as if I'd been beaten, because the blood thinner that I was taking caused easy bruising.

The physical and emotional trauma of this incident made both

Jeannie and me question, *Oh, my God, why me? What did I do to piss you off?*

I was admitted from the ER to the hospital that Saturday instead of Monday. We proceeded with the ventricular ablation, which thankfully was a success.

After that, Jeannie and I committed to living a normal life while continuing our upward career trajectories. In 2004, Hugh Greeley again facilitated that, while speaking with his friend and colleague, Kent Wallace, who was then Senior Vice President of Operations at Vanguard Health Systems. Today he is Chief Operating Officer for Kindred Healthcare Systems.

Kent had told Hugh that he was looking for a Chief Medical Officer.

Hugh immediately responded: "Herman Williams is your guy."

Kent and I had spoken many times before by phone about consulting work that I was doing with his hospitals for The Greeley Company. In fact, our introduction had involved a volatile situation with a doctor at a hospital in Selma, Alabama.

"What was perfect," Kent recalls, "was the fact that Herman was this unbelievably sharp, well-educated man who would sit and connect in that community. This doctor was just totally off the deep end. Herman's presence was divine intervention, due to his credibility as a doctor, and one of his greatest skills is that he's a very calming individual. He has one of the most gentle spirits of anybody that I know. As a result, he handled this situation very effectively."

My track record of positive resolutions for several contentious situations like this inspired Kent to invite me to interview to oversee five hospitals in San Antonio that were run by the Baptist Health System, which was owned by Vanguard Health.

"When Herman came down and interviewed," Kent says, "he and I clicked, and he clicked with the new team. Most importantly, when the medical staff members interviewed Herman, he just knocked it out of the park."

I was hired as Chief Medical Officer for the five-hospital Baptist Health System. On my first day, Kent handed me a book called *Execution: The Discipline of Getting Things Done* by Lawrence Bossidy and Ram Charan.

"I want you to read this book," Kent said. "So many people have great strategies. They're really smart, but they don't know how to execute on the strategy."

This was the first of many invaluable lessons I learned from Kent. And to this day, my mantra is, "Can you execute it? Success is all about execution."

One of my first assignments was to work with Hugh to transform a hospital system whose leadership was in disarray. We had to create a new governance group for five facilities. One was the oldest medical center downtown, which was viewed as the 800-pound gorilla; the other four facilities felt powerless. Hugh and I created a new medical staff structure, and we needed the 2,500 physicians on staff to vote to pass it by changing the bylaws. After a year of assembling the program, we managed to get about 900 physicians to vote to implement our plan.

"That turnout was extraordinary," Kent says, "and it was a real testament to how Herman put them together. It was a great start for us because he established immediate credibility and that gave me the utmost confidence in Herman's abilities."

Fast forward to 2007, and my confidence in my health was so strong, I became a little cocky and cavalier about taking my medication and getting regular lab work. Four years had passed since my last shock. That led to becoming a bad patient. In December of 2007, I told my doctor that I'd been having runs of accelerated heart rate.

The nurse warned, "Go get your blood drawn to check your potassium. It may be low, and that would be dangerous."

Feeling invincible, I ignored her orders and decided to get my blood drawn in a week when it was more convenient. My noncompliance caught up with me one sunny Sunday morning at the country club, before a round of golf with my best friend's father. I felt fine as we got out of the car.

"Thamir," I said, "wait in the cart. I'm going to get us signed in."

"Okay," he said.

I ran into the club to sign us in for nine holes of golf, but on my way back down the stairs—

Bam!

A shock stopped me in my tracks. Here I was, frozen with fear and pain in the back staircase on a Sunday morning, with no one around. Thamir was too far away to hear me.

My heart kept pounding away… and it was fast! Then, as if by divine intervention, a woman appeared out of nowhere. I gave her my keys and said, "Please go to my car and get the black bag out of the trunk."

The bag contained my emergency magnet, which I had received from my doctor in Beaumont. When held to my chest, the magnet would render the defibrillator ineffective and prevent it from shocking me. Since I had been awake for essentially every shock except for one during the last 16 years, we felt it was acceptable to use the magnet, as long as I was awake. If I passed out, I would essentially drop the magnet and the device would do its job. Even though I was now in San Antonio, I kept the magnet in my bag for emergencies like this.

The woman returned with the bag. I retrieved the magnet, which I held to my chest. Unfortunately, with the defibrillator de-activated, my heart raced out of control. I passed out on top of the magnet.

The next thing I knew, the most wonderful sense of peace overwhelmed me. While my body was sprawled on the stairs, my mind was in a dream-like state, where I was riding down the street in a convertible yellow Cadillac, staring up at palm trees as a Roberta Flack song played.

"Herman! Herman!"

A paramedic was calling me back to consciousness, but I didn't want to come back, because I felt so serene. When I finally woke up, I was looking up at a country club employee who had just given me CPR, along with members of the San Antonio Fire Department. Meanwhile, the country club had called Jeannie to notify her of the incident, and Thamir remained in the golf cart, wondering why people were running around as a fire truck and ambulance arrived in my absence.

Jeannie and Cole arrived at the scene. While in San Antonio, Jeannie was working three days each week as a dental hygienist. She also volunteered as a room parent at Cole's school, where she was exposed to and contracted "Fifth Disease." That triggered a painful, full-body arthritis which devastated Jeannie's hands, making her unable to practice dental hygiene and forcing her to retire in 2008. On top of that, Jeannie suffered from Crohn's disease, which is aggravated by stress. As always, she exhibited grace under pressure by enduring her own physical pain while tending to my many crises.

For this crisis, Cole was devastated. It was the first time he was old enough to witness one of my health emergencies. He says now, "If you think something bad is happening with your parents, it's like the end of the world."

At the hospital, doctors confirmed that my potassium was dangerously low. Had I been a compliant patient by getting it checked, this terrifying episode could have been avoided. Lesson learned. Oh! Did I mention that my doc was furious with me, and that he confiscated my magnet? I returned to work, determined to take better care of myself.

Meanwhile, Kent was promoted to President and Chief Operating Officer, and transferred to the Vanguard Health Systems corporate offices in Nashville. He honored his promise to take me to Nashville if an opportunity became available. He made that happen, by creating a role for me as Vice President of Medical Affairs, and bringing me to Nashville in February of 2009.

Kent says, "Herman's job was to run physician leadership groups across America to influence people to let them know that our hospital CEOs want to hear and resolve problems that physicians were having. This involved nearly 500 physicians at more than 25 hospitals. The problem was that physicians felt CEOs did not listen to their irritants, nor did the CEOs implement solutions. Herman created a national environment to do that. Herman can move across all lines of individuals in the hospital. It's like he's taken his gentle bedside manner as a physician into conference rooms where he can heal administrative and management conflicts as a conciliator or facilitator. And that's what makes him so successful at what he does."

All was well as I created my new dream of becoming a successful physician executive. I had all but forgotten about the Kerlan Clinic dream. The sights and sounds of being a doctor were only a memory, such as treating femur fractures in the trauma center, and hearing the constant beat of helicopter blades as new patients were brought to the ED via Life Flight. Those were the days.

Sadly, life brought more loss on March 11, 2011, when my father died at age 83. The cause, ironically, was pulmonary fibrosis, which was the potential side effect of the lifesaving drug that I had been taking since 1995. I delivered the eulogy at his funeral, and I'm including an excerpt in the Appendix of this book. While I miss my father terribly, I am at peace with the belief that I have truly become the Renaissance Man that he had envisioned for my life.

The definition of renaissance is "rebirth or revival." How ironic that I had come to epitomize that persona in ways that neither I nor my father would have ever fathomed as I was growing up. This continued to prove true as my career progressed after his passing. Now, as I reflect on his influence, he was always there for me, always supportive and loving.

Despite losing my father, life was good for me and Jeannie. In 2012, five years after my last shock, my health was stable when I saw my doctor at a routine cardiology appointment. He suggested that I stop taking the blood thinner Coumadin, which had been prescribed since my cardiac arrest. He recommended that I take aspirin instead. His suggestion was based on a recent article in *The New England Journal of Medicine*[1] that said aspirin was just as effective as Coumadin as adjunctive therapy in heart failure patients who were in normal sinus rhythm.

Since I was a heart failure patient with a normal heart rate and rhythm, it appeared that I was a candidate for taking aspirin instead of Coumadin. So, after a careful discussion of the risks and benefits, as well as the chance to stop having my blood drawn every six weeks while on Coumadin, we decided to switch to coated aspirin. For six months, I had no problems. Unfortunately, in February of 2013, the aspirin took its toll on my stomach. Severe pain landed me in the emergency room.

---

1   Shunichi Homma, MD, John L.P. Thompson, Ph.D., *Warfarin and Aspirin in Patients with Heart Failure and Sinus Rhythm*, N Engl J Med 2012; 366:1859-1869

"Herman, stop taking the aspirin right away," my doctor said. "Let's wait a week and figure out what to do."

That seemed like a great plan. For the next week, I was fine — and grateful that life seemed back to normal. In fact, Jeannie and I were on a support group panel where we discussed the topic of cardiac patients who'd had strokes. We left the event thinking, *Thank God this is not an issue for us.* A stroke would be my worst nightmare, and thankfully the Coumadin had mitigated the risk all these years. That evening, we hosted a Valentine's Day dinner at our house and enjoyed a wonderful celebration of life and love with our friends. We went to bed feeling normal.

But something was gravely wrong when I awoke the next morning at 6:15 on February 18, 2013.

I jumped out of bed — and almost fell over. I couldn't stand. I knew immediately, thanks to my medical training, that I was having a stroke. I tried to shout, "Jeannie!" But an unintelligible sound came from my mouth.

She turned on a lamp and ran around our king-sized bed. As I stood on wobbly legs, she appeared to be coming toward me in slow motion. Immediately recognizing the classic signs of a stroke, including slurred speech, she sat me on a vanity bench in the bathroom, then ran upstairs to get Cole.

"Daddy's not feeling well," she told him. "Throw on your clothes. We have to take him to the hospital."

When Jeannie returned, my symptoms had worsened. Cole stayed with me while she called 911 in the next room. Then she discovered me and Cole in the closet.

"What is this?" Jeannie demanded as I put on a button-down shirt and jeans. "Why are you getting dressed up to go in an ambulance?"

When the ambulance arrived, it took them a little longer to get me situated, and 15 minutes later I finally left for the ER. Cole decided to stay with a neighbor. At the hospital, the attending physician told us that an MRI was the best procedure to evaluate the extent of a stroke. However, I told him that I had a defibrillator and we both realized that people with defibrillators can't get near an MRI due to the incredible magnetic field and the possibility of reprogramming the defibrillator.

"Okay," the doctor said, taking a long pause. "The next best test is a CT scan with contrast."

However, due to my decreased kidney function secondary to my cardiac arrest in 1991, they were afraid to administer the dye, since it could shut down my kidneys. As if that weren't enough, we also determined that I was not a candidate for any "clot-busting" medication, which must be given within three hours of the onset of a stroke. We did not know the time of the onset of the stroke.

Then, to my horror, an echocardiogram revealed a three-centimeter clot in the lower chamber of the right ventricle of my heart. The only treatment that I was a candidate for was the blood thinner Heparin, delivered via IV. This would dissolve the clot and give my body a chance to resolve this on its own. I was admitted into the Neuro-ICU, and all we could do was wait for the final outcomes. My life was in God's hands.

This presented my sixth major life challenge: surviving a health crisis involving another organ system. That's how physicians think — in terms of "organ systems." As you injure one, it trips into another, triggering a devastating domino effect on overall health. So, having heart problems which lead to lung problems can then cause kidney problems and other neurological problems, all of which work together to march the human body closer toward a diminished quality of life, and ultimately, death.

Jeannie, of course, was excruciatingly aware of this, and we found ourselves in that familiar place of panic and terror about whether I would pull through, and if so, in what condition.

CHAPTER EIGHT

The Awakening

JEANNIE PRAYED INTENSELY THAT I would weather this new crisis unscathed. God heard her; Heparin dissolved the clot within three days. My speech returned to normal. Doctors started me back on my original blood thinner, Coumadin.

"Herman," the doctors told us, "it looks like no damage was done to your brain."

"Oh, thank God!" I exclaimed.

I was 55 years old, and I had survived another catastrophic illness. But this time, I didn't fling open the doors to the boisterous pity party that I'd been hosting inside my head for more than two decades. My mind didn't reverberate with woeful cries of *God, why me?*

I just couldn't go there this time. Jeannie was constantly expressing joy and marveling that I was okay. As was my lifelong friend, Phil Morris, who has pursued a very spiritual path throughout his Los Angeles-based acting career. He reminded me that my ability to survive and thrive despite life-threatening circumstances should be viewed as a blessing, not a curse.

Suddenly, an epiphany struck me like an apple falling out of a tree.

"Whoa!" I exclaimed. "I get it now!"

In that moment, I felt my mind, my heart, and my spirit all simultaneously open like giant camera shutters, enabling me to see life through an entirely new lens.

Everything became CLEAR! for the first time, as I awakened to the thrilling realization that my original dream of becoming an orthopedic surgeon to the stars had died for a reason. God had a bigger plan for my life. And that was to first bring me to a consciousness about my life's purpose, and then to show me that He had deliberately prepared me to embark on an altruistic mission of helping people in ways that I had never imaged. As Phil and I talked, this new clarity overwhelmed me with emotion and goosebumps.

"Phil, I get it now," I said. "I'm supposed to use the extraordinary circumstances of my life story to teach as many people who will listen about the precious nature of life; the fact is that we don't live forever, but we have control over our joy in life."

From that moment on, I found immense, overwhelming joy in the simple things that I had been doing for years and years: hugging Cole; waking up beside Jeannie and loving that we had a whole new day ahead of us; greeting strangers in the elevator at work; savoring a sweet, creamy cup of steaming coffee; enjoying the warm sunshine on my face.

I loved the feeling of simply being alive. Breathing, walking, talking, encountering people at work, greeting complete strangers in public, marveling at the majesty of nature, relishing the taste of delicious food, being acutely aware of the joy of laughing or playing music. The list is endless. I began to clearly understand what the late author and poet Maya Angelou said: "Life is not measured by the number of breaths we take, but by the moments that take our breath away."

Suddenly, as I awakened to my life's true purpose and passion, countless moments every day were taking my breath away. And it made me wonder, *How I could have lived any other way?*

How could I have, for so many years, allowed the curse of negative thinking to rob me of appreciating the countless blessings being showered on me all day long? And how could I teach this to others, before they looked back on decades with regret that they had not seized every opportunity to truly enjoy life? How could I use my experience to help others live in compassion and gratitude — even if they had never suffered a cardiac arrest, or health catastrophes, or major problems of any kind, for that matter? Was it necessary to survive great suffering in order to awaken to the joy and thankfulness that I was now experiencing?

I had to let these questions percolate in my spirit for a few years before I could craft an action plan. One thing was clear: I had reached the "acceptance" phase of Elizabeth Kübler-Ross' Five Stages of Grief. I was at peace with what had happened to me, and how it had dramatically changed the course of my life. So now what was I supposed to do with that?

For starters, I celebrated that Jeannie and I had instilled our altruistic values into our son, Cole. I tell Cole now, "You're here for a reason, and I want you to be true to yourself. Hopefully you can look beyond these distractions and keep your eyes on the prize."

Cole, who is 21 and studying at Case Western Reserve University, says that my precarious health status enables him to deeply appreciate people in the moment.

"You have to value people and whatever you hold dear when you have it," Cole explains, "because you never know when it will go away. You have to be kind, because you never know what someone is going through. You never know if that's the last time you'll see them. You have to value their existence and presence. I learned from my dad that every day could be the last day that I see him. Every time I talk with him, I try to be nice and see him off with a smile."

Jeannie and I have also taught Cole to help others by creating a positive environment when possible.

"One day," Cole recalls, "we were driving to get dinner and we saw an accident. I said, 'I'm going to help,' and I got out to help. My dad taught me, you never know what you can do in a given situation until you've investigated what all your options are. I put myself in danger to help someone I didn't know."

Likewise, our family experience — and years of living in terror that a deadly cardiac arrest could strike again, suddenly, and without warning — has deepened Jeannie's faith.

"I try not to take anything for granted," she says. "I try to live one day at time. I put my faith in God and do what I have to do. It makes you realize how delicate and precious life really is. Basically, he died, and they brought him back. He was lucky."

Jeannie finds meaning and purpose in being forced to create a new dream. "There's a reason why Herman needed this path. Practicing medicine was not his path. God puts you where you're supposed to be. Yes, bad things happen. We get through it and hopefully learn from it. Hopefully that pulls you closer to Him in your spiritual growth."

Looking back on my life, I see and feel that God has spoken to me through people. My parents raised me to believe I could be and do anything, even when my behavior and performance seemed to jeopardize my better judgment. Jeannie showed me unconditional love and nursed me back to health. My brother Bill and my friend Phil always did and said what I needed in that moment, while making me laugh and pulling me through the toughest times. Cole has enabled me to enjoy the immeasurable, indescribable love that a parent has for a child. And many mentors have helped me become who I am today.

When contacted for this book, Richard Williams, Don Parks, Gus White, Hugh Greeley, and Kent Wallace each admitted: "I didn't know the impact I was having on Herman at the time."

Gus White specifically told me to "Pay it Forward!" That means, we all get help from someone, and we should all look back and help someone else in need.

So, I now say, "Pay It Forward by Reaching Backwards."

Therein lies a huge life lesson: be kind to everyone, and use your knowledge and resources to help people, because you could dramatically change the course of their lives without even knowing it. You could be as Dr. Williams and Dr. Parks were for me, showing that yes, a black man can become a physician. You could be as Dr. White was, sharing his knowledge, his friends, and his stature, by inviting me to publish a prestigious article with him and believing I could become an orthopedic surgeon. You could be like Hugh Greeley, taking me under his wing to groom me for excellence in a career that I had never considered. And you could emulate Kent Wallace, who opened doors to corporate leadership positions that have enabled me to help improve healthcare for thousands of people — as well as usher more people of color through those doors behind me.

These men showed me that helping people transcends race. Donald Parks, Richard Williams, and Gus White are African American. Kent Wallace and Hugh Greeley are Caucasian. Each of them saw something in me that they identified with, and that inspired them to help me. As a result, I mentor men and women of all races.

My current position as Executive Vice President and Chief Clinical Officer at RCCH Healthcare Partners allows me to help improve healthcare for people across America. That ability has steadily increased since my first hospital operations job when I was taking care of one hospital; I now oversee Quality and Clinical Operations for 17 facilities.

Having risen from that devastating moment when I realized I could not be an orthopedic surgeon — to the honor of serving in this position — exemplifies the power of helping people. I wouldn't be here without Kent Wallace's continuous orchestration of my ascent to RCCH Healthcare Partners. I would not have reached that point without Hugh Greeley's training. And without the influence of Richard Williams, Don Parks, and Gus White, I may not have reached the pinnacle of my medical training where I was the day I died on April 28, 1991.

Now, as I celebrate 26 years of living a new dream and enjoying an awakening about how I lived to tell about it, I humbly offer a framework for living and appreciating life. It's called *The ABCs of Life*. It is my blueprint for building a better day for yourself, your loved ones, and complete strangers alike to cultivate peace, joy, prosperity, and health.

God gave me the gift of a second lifetime, a new dream, and the ability to find meaning in it all. The magic of that is woven into my tools, such as *The Kindness Scale*, which is explained in the last chapter. It is my gift to you.

CHAPTER NINE

How To Get Clear On Your Purpose

To Live The Life You Didn't Dream Of

"CLEAR!"

That's what paramedics and doctors exclaim before placing defibrillator paddles on the chest of a patient in cardiac arrest.

"CLEAR!" warns everyone to move away from the patient, to avoid being harmed by the loud, electric jolt that shoots through the paddles, jolts the body, and hopefully jumpstarts the heart.

Of course, the paramedics warned "CLEAR!" before attempting to shock me as I lay lifeless on the gymnasium floor on April 28, 1991. As you recall, the defibrillator malfunctioned. No electric shock was given. The symbolism of that failed attempt at saving my life is profound. It testifies to the perseverance of my friends who continued CPR while awaiting the arrival of a functioning defibrillator. And as every passing second diminished my chances for survival, the paramedics' echo of "CLEAR!" in the silent gymnasium also illuminated the power of fate and faith.

My fate — whether I would live or remain dead — was entirely in God's hands. He chose to keep me alive, and I chose to believe that He had a powerful purpose for my future. Even though that purpose remained obscured as years of pain, fear, depression, and health crises blinded me to what good could possibly result from being robbed of my lifetime dream.

However, I persevered on the deep faith that my parents had instilled in me from birth, as well as the belief that this trauma couldn't possibly have happened to me as some cruel coincidence. Deep down, I trusted that there was a greater plan for my life.

Sometimes the most difficult dilemmas, life-crushing catastrophes, and seemingly impossible situations serve as catalysts to awaken us into new, better ways of thinking, feeling, and living.

"The wound is the place where the Light enters you," the great poet Rumi once wrote. Light symbolizes awakening to your best self in mind, body, and spirit. Without the wound, the pain, and the grueling recovery, that enlightenment might never occur. I have discovered that something extremely powerful results from enduring trauma, pain, fear, and life-threatening crisis.

For me, that result is clarity of purpose — as God ordained, not as we humans attempt to conceive for ourselves. That is the essence of this book. The value of my life story illustrates that whatever you're enduring right now, you can ascend to an extremely fulfilling, prosperous, healthy, and joyous life. It was only during the course of surviving a cardiac arrest, dozens of shocks, and a stroke, that I was blessed with the lucidity to see a higher purpose for my life. It is not the life that I dreamed of. It is the life that was predestined for me, and I trust that with every heartbeat.

That's why this book is called "CLEAR!" Because suffering enabled me to clearly see my life's purpose, and how to derive pleasure from it for myself and everyone I encounter each day.

The tragedies that could have crushed my mind, body, and spirit actually empowered me to think, live, love, and work in ways that were unfathomable before April 28, 1991. The past 26 years of pain and challenges refined me into someone who is awed by the simple joys of life, while cherishing my family and friends, and doing professional work that helps thousands of people heal and thrive across America every day.

I have also come to marvel that the breadth and depth of God's vision for my life vastly exceeds anything I could have possibly created or comprehended prior to my resuscitation from sudden death by cardiac arrest.

Now I am sharing this knowledge with you as a gift. In this chapter, you can do exercises and take action steps to live with the same joy, purpose, and passion that I cherish all day, every day. I call these exercises and action steps my Clear Prescriptions for Living the Life You Didn't Dream Of. They are:

CLEAR Rx #1   Get Clear with The Four Themes of
               Surviving & Thriving

CLEAR Rx #2   Write Your Personal Mission Statement

CLEAR Rx #3   Apply The ABCs of Life

CLEAR Rx #4   Utilize The ABCs of Leadership

CLEAR Rx #5   Commit Everyday Actions for
               Compassionate Living with The Kindness
               Scale

For Living the Life You Didn't Dream Of

Get Clear with The Four Themes of Surviving & Thriving

FOUR KEY THEMES FORMED a framework for my ability to survive and thrive after the physical and emotional trauma of sudden death by cardiac arrest. Now you can apply these truths to persevere through life's toughest challenges.

The Four Themes of Surviving & Thriving

1. Believe in something bigger than yourself.

2. Know that your Higher Power, God, Buddha, the Universe, or your spiritual entity, has a greater plan for your life than you can conceive for yourself.

3. Understand that suffering is a relative experience and that resilience always trumps pain.

4. Appreciate and accept that the unwavering devotion of your loved ones can provide you with the power to prevail.

For me, my wife's unwavering devotion empowered me to heal and triumph over the trauma of illness and my device.

1. Believe in something bigger than yourself.

This was key to surviving because I often felt helpless to improve my situation. However, even when trauma was blinding me early on, my deep faith in God, and belief that there was a divine plan for my life, enabled me to trust that my experience had a purpose that would be revealed someday.

What do you believe in that's bigger than yourself?

_____

_____

_____

_____

_____

How does faith in this Higher Power strengthen you to endure and overcome pain, obstacles, and difficult circumstances?

_____

_____

_____

_____

_____

How can you deepen this belief?

_____

_____

_____

_____

_____

2. Know that there is a greater plan for your life than you can conceive for yourself.

This belief allowed me to endure those early treatment challenges, such as finding the correct medication and getting repeatedly defibrillated. Despite the painful chaos of my daily reality, I knew that I would find light at the end of the tunnel. All I had to do was persevere through the tunnel.

What is the dream that you created for yourself?

_____

_____

_____

_____

_____

Describe how your injury, loss, illness, tragedy, trauma, or disappointing circumstances shattered that dream.

_____

_____

_____

_____

_____

What greater plan do you think exists for your life by forcing you to endure this crisis or catastrophe?

_____

_____

_____

_____

_____

How has your situation given you the clarity to create a new dream for your life?

_____

_____

_____

_____

_____

3. Understand that suffering is a relative experience and that resilience always trumps pain.

The pain of the shocks was a temporary experience, and I believed that we would ultimately discover a medication to effectively control my heart rate. All I had to do was stay resilient and believe. I also realized that suffering is a relative experience. Your worst suffering might seem enviable to someone else. For example, the person who's waiting for an organ transplant might view my health challenges as a minor inconvenience compared to lying in a hospital bed as their time ticks toward death until a life-saving organ is available.

Most recently, a bout with pneumonia had me coughing and feeling miserable, but I realized, it can always be worse. A person who is enduring the breathing difficulties of incurable emphysema might covet the temporary and curable discomfort of pneumonia. Keeping that in mind enabled me to focus on gratitude that antibiotics and rest would enable me to feel better very soon. We can't make value judgments on suffering because it's a personal experience. Suffering for one person may not be so for someone else. This belief fuels our resilience to succeed.

How can you apply the belief that suffering is a relative experience to view your challenges in a way that makes them easier to accept and endure?

_____

_____

_____

_____

_____

How can you recast your thinking to mitigate your suffering through the lens that things can always be worse, and that one person's pain might be another person's mere inconvenience?

_____

_____

_____

_____

_____

Since resilience always trumps pain, what can you tell yourself in order to persevere and believe that everything will work out for the best?

_____

_____

_____

_____

_____

How can you avoid thinking that pain trumps resilience, which will make you succumb to the pain and remain stuck in misery?

_____

_____

_____

_____

_____

4. Appreciate that your loved ones' unconditional love can provide the power to prevail.

Your loved ones can help you immeasurably. For me, my wife's unwavering devotion empowered me to heal and triumph over the trauma of illness and my defibrillator. Jeannie's unconditional love and inexhaustible care, despite fear for my emotional and physical well-being, was instrumental to my ability to recover on every level. Had it not been for her support, I do not believe that I would have triumphed over this on-going crisis.

For you, this means accepting and appreciating assistance from people who want to help you, and seeking support if you don't already have it.

Who in your life provides unconditional love?

_____

_____

_____

_____

_____

How does that person's unconditional love empower you to persevere through challenges?

_____

_____

_____

_____

_____

Where could you go, or what could you do, to seek support and create a compassionate and supportive network around yourself?

_____

_____

_____

_____

_____

Do you resist accepting help due to pride, shame, or fear? How can you release those negative feelings and receive life-giving assistance?

_____

_____

_____

_____

_____

How can you show this person or these people how much you appreciate their support that is enabling you to cope, heal, succeed, and create a new dream for your life?

_____

_____

_____

_____

_____

For Living the Life You Didn't Dream Of

Write Your Personal Mission Statement

ANSWERING THE QUESTIONS IN the previous section enabled me to gain a clear understanding of my life's purpose, and how to apply it, so I could live life to the fullest. That inspired me to compose this Personal Mission Statement:

> *My reason for living is to make sure that everyone I*
> *encounter is better off in some way when they leave me.*

That simple sentence captures how I approach every interaction with Jeannie, Cole, my mother, Bill, Phil, friends, family members, colleagues, and strangers. All I can do is *try* to achieve that, whether it's by doing something as simple as giving a compliment; or as involved as mentoring a young person to excel in college and a career; or as complicated as resolving a major bureaucratic issue with hospitals.

If you believe in karma, then you'll be quick to recognize the immense power of living with compassion and kindness every day. Karma is a spiritual principle of cause and effect; everything you do has a ripple effect in the universe. If you do something good, positive experiences will boomerang back on you; if you do something bad, negative circumstances will plague you.

The beauty is that leaving people better off will cost you absolutely nothing, and can be achieved in the split-second required to smile or nod at someone. By blessing another person with a kind gesture, you are actually blessing yourself and many others.

Ancient spiritual principles promise that we reap what we sow, and that is absolutely true with kindness. Research proves that the person who initiates an act of kindness is rewarded with as much joy — or even more — than the person receiving it. Therefore, the more you give, the more you receive. Let me tell you: this keeps me flying high all day long, constantly fueling my spirit with the happiness I feel when I do or say something nice.

This particular mission statement was inspired by my suffering, and enables me to express the wellspring of love that has replaced the gloom, PTSD, fear, and paralyzing depression that once plagued me.

Clearly, a Personal Mission Statement summarizes your purpose and lays a foundation for how you live, work, and play. Think about your own Personal Mission Statement. Whether you have endured trauma and tragedy, or whether your life has been smooth sailing, what do you believe is the highest purpose for your existence? What do you think you were put here on earth to accomplish in ways that help you, your family, your community, and the world?

Keep in mind that your life purpose does not have to be something as grandiose as winning the Nobel Peace Prize or ending world hunger. Dr. Martin Luther King, Jr. once said, "If a man is called to be a street sweeper, he should sweep streets even as a Michelangelo painted, or Beethoven composed music or Shakespeare wrote poetry. He should sweep streets so well that all the hosts of heaven and earth will pause to say, 'Here lived a great street sweeper who did his job well.'"

Listen to your heart's deepest desires. Do you dream of opening a bakery to sell the cakes and pies that everyone raves about? Do you long to write a novel? Have you survived extraordinary circumstances and want to teach others how you did it? Did you discover an elixir that everyday people can use to feel better? Do you simply want to be the best parent, friend, teacher, coach, employee, etc.?

Considering all of this, write one sentence summarizing your life mission.

My Personal Mission Statement is:

_____

_____

_____

_____

_____

If at first you have trouble composing your Personal Mission Statement, be patient with yourself. You can begin by simply jotting down a few core ideas. Pray and meditate on them, then come back to revise them as your spirit guides you. Allow these concepts to crystallize in your mind. You will eventually be ready to write your official Personal Mission Statement.

Meanwhile, you can begin to incorporate my Clear Prescriptions for Living the Life You Didn't Dream Of. They will help you elevate your mind, body, and spirit into a whole new realm of peace, purpose, and prosperity. An abundant life is your reward for following actions that are inspired by your heart's deepest desires.

After I identified my Personal Mission Statement, I continued to reinvent myself by creating a model for how to execute my life's mission. This model consists of three parts:

The ABCs of Life

The ABCs of Leadership

The Kindness Scale

I am providing *The ABCs of Life, The ABCs of Leadership, and The Kindness Scale* so you may apply them to gain deeper clarity about your purpose, then live the life that you didn't dream of, despite disappointments, disease, and catastrophes that may have killed your desires for your life. I hope that these Clear Prescriptions can help you realize the divine plan that a Higher Power is orchestrating for you, especially when honed through challenges and crises.

At the same time, I pray that you can utilize my tools to soar through life without having to suffer as I did. I have often wondered: *Can life's most profound insights only be discovered through deep suffering? Would I have conceived The ABCs of Life, The ABCs of Leadership, and The Kindness Scale while living my original dream as an orthopedic surgeon?*

I'll never know for sure, but my hunch is that I would not.

For Living the Life You Didn't Dream Of

Apply The ABCs of Life

WHEN PARAMEDICS, DOCTORS, AND everyday people learn how to perform cardiopulmonary resuscitation, they're taught an easy way to remember how to focus and proceed with simplicity and speed to save a life. If you find someone on the ground unconscious, you assess the airway, check for breathing, and evaluate blood circulation. Thus, the three key words for CPR are:

Airway, Breathing, and Circulation.

These are the ABCs of CPR, and they saved my life. The resuscitation of my body, as well as my way of thinking, living, and working inspired me to create *The ABCs of Life*, which are:

Acknowledgement, Breathing, and Compassion.

When you apply *The ABCs of Life* in conjunction with *The Kindness Scale*, you can chart a course to a new dream for your life on every level. I created the following chart to illustrate how this works; an explanation follows.

The ABCs of Life...

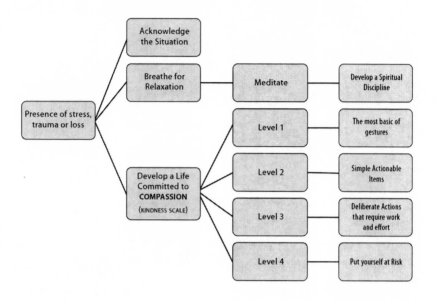

THE ABCS OF LIFE:

A IS FOR ACKNOWLEDGEMENT

> *"I woke up every morning acknowledging that I was not the same person as I was prior to my cardiac arrest. Not as strong, incredibly vulnerable, literally a cardiac cripple... but all the while, REFUSING to be defined by a stereotype."*
>
> — *Herman Williams, MD*

I had to *acknowledge* the physical and professional limitations that my health crisis imposed on me. Like it or not: what you resist persists. If you dwell on the problem, the pain, and the changes it forces you to make, you will never free your mind or spirit to ascend into a new way of thinking to conceive a fresh strategy for your life. Regret, resentment, and anger block you from becoming your best self.

Had I expended time and energy on denying that my life was irreversibly changed, I would have stayed stuck or spiraled further downward into depression, mental stagnation, and career catastrophe. Instead, I *acknowledged* that I had a severe cardiac abnormality and that I would have to compensate to create the most normal life possible. Once I *acknowledged* the limitations of my heart, I was ready to make decisions about which treatment options I would be willing to undergo.

I also *acknowledged* that I would never be a practicing orthopedic surgeon. I faced that reality with my father's oft-repeated words in mind: "Everything works out the way it's supposed to be." There was something with a greater purpose for me.

I had no idea what that was, but I trusted that God had a good reason for my miraculous resuscitation. After all, I was dead. Yet He orchestrated the experience in ways that enabled me to survive. If a cardiac arrest had occurred while I was alone, you would not be reading this book. I would be dead.

Acknowledging and feeling grateful for the miraculous circumstances that God synchronized to ensure my survival deepens my faith that He made this happen for a reason. It was my job to believe that, and to stay in a positive mindset so that I could recognize exactly how I was supposed to use this experience to help others.

When you *acknowledge* your condition, you realize that we're all here for a reason. At the most basic premise, we're here to improve the value of life. Using the power of deliberate breathing, coupled with meditation, you can make a spiritual connection that enables you to live a life of compassion. That enables me to peacefully *acknowledge* that my condition could someday, maybe, require me to need a heart transplant. I will cross that bridge if my life journey takes me there. I refuse to worry about it now; I am too busy loving my life today. Achieving the ability to practice mindfulness — or focusing on "the here and now" as opposed to the past or future — is the key to cultivating peace and joy in everything we do.

The country song, *Live Like You Were Dying*, written by Tim Nichols and Craig Wiseman, expresses my philosophy of savoring every second of every day as if it could be our last. It very well could be, and suffering from a serious health condition like mine makes me especially cognizant of that fact.

To reach this peaceful way of thinking, you have to *acknowledge* that something really bad happened to you. Then *acknowledge* the implications and the consequences. That *acknowledgement* defines what you are going to do to change your mindset. If you've had a stroke and are paralyzed, you can't change that. But you can impact the way you're going to live your life. Ask yourself: *Am I going to define myself by this? What can I do? What can't I do? And what will I do with my life now that something terrible has happened? What are some ways I can enjoy my daily existence, for example, after a terminal cancer diagnosis?*

Whatever your crisis may be, here are some exercises to delve deeper into how you can design the best possible outcome.

Acknowledge: I am in charge of how I respond to this challenge. Describe the best ways that you can face your circumstances. What thoughts, actions, and strategies can you use every day to help you cope, recover, and excel in ways that help you evolve into an even stronger person?

Write a description of yourself responding to your challenge in the most positive, peaceful, and resourceful manner possible. Include specific examples, such as, "When I am overwhelmed by physical pain, I list all the blessings that I'm thankful for, such as, I am thankful for the love of my family. I am thankful for a warm, safe place for us to live. I am thankful for my life being spared. I am thankful for the ability to find meaning and purpose in this pain in ways that help myself and others."

If you're going through a frightening life transition, write a description of yourself feeling and acting with courage, assertiveness, and self-confidence.

Acknowledge: I will recruit the best people to help me cope and thrive, especially family, friends, and caregivers. *Make a list of the people who love you unconditionally and will want to help you without hesitation.*

Compile a list of resources that can help you, such as transportation, special services, and programs. Make a plan to apply for and utilize these resources in ways that facilitate your ability to cope with your crisis.

Acknowledge: "I will allow myself time to mourn, but will not give in to my crisis and will not allow this situation to define me." Declare that. Now write a plan for how you can do this.

_____

_____

_____

_____

Acknowledge: I understand that everyone eventually leaves this earthly existence, and I will seek to enjoy every minute with love for others. Explain how you will do that every day.

_____

_____

_____

_____

_____

Acknowledge: I will enjoy more loving moments with family and friends. Explain how you will do this daily.

_____

_____

_____

_____

_____

THE ABCs OF LIFE:

B IS FOR BREATHE

> *"If you achieve a certain stability of breath, the static of your psychological and circumstantial activities will diminish and open up a phenomenal clarity."*
>
> — *Sadhguru Jaggi Vasudev*
> *Founder of the ISHA Foundation*

THE ANCIENT SANSKRIT WORD for breath is "life." Your breath is literally your life. Without oxygen, the brain and body die. Fortunately, *breathing* occurs automatically; we don't have to think about it. But when we *do* think about our breathing, we can make magic happen for our minds, bodies, and spirits.

Breathing has become a powerful tool for me every day to control my mood and well-being on every level. I have been cultivating this skill for years since I learned to meditate, which focuses on the breath.

That's why the "B" in *The ABCs of Life* is for *Breathe*. It represents the many relaxation techniques that begin with a single, slow, deep breath.

Once I *acknowledged* that my disease was susceptible to subtle increases in my stress level, I used relaxation to deal with the bumps in the road. In most situations, breathing and relaxation were extremely therapeutic. Every time I had an episode of a rapid heart rate or defibrillation, I always tried to relax by using a *breathing* technique. I also used psychological biofeedback that I learned years ago to calm myself back toward a normal heart rate.

As I learned more about the meaning of breathing and the

importance of relaxation, I discovered the practice of meditation. While yearning for a better understanding of meditation, I discovered the Isha Foundation. I attended several seminars sponsored by this nonprofit organization. The Isha Foundation is devoted to the practice of meditation and the discovery of its healing benefits. Their mission statement is as follows:

> *Isha Foundation is dedicated to raising human consciousness, and fosters global harmony through individual transformation. Guided by Sadhguru, it is an essential resource for exploring the ancient science of yoga in all its depth and dimensions. The foundation offers a variety of programs that provide methods for anyone to attain physical, mental, and spiritual wellbeing. Its offerings allow participants to deepen their experience of life, and reach their ultimate potential.*

Sadhguru described it best when he said this about *breathing*: "Having a certain mastery over one's breath can change the fundamental chemistry to bring about pleasantness of experience of health, joy, and ecstasy from within."

Breathing is the essence of life, meditation, and relaxation. *Breathing* helps you stay centered, and when you augment that with meditation, it calms your spirit. That enables you to deal with life's heavy-duty joy-crushers such as resentment, animosity, dog-eat-dog competition, disease, disappointment, and defeat.

With each inhalation and exhalation, my alpha and beta waves changed. They slowed. My heart rate decelerated as well. So now, if I feel my heart rate accelerating, I take deep, focused *breaths*. The act of performing this simple action gives your brain something to do instead of exploding into a panic of thoughts about a potentially difficult situation. Focused *breathing* enables you to distract yourself from whatever stressful circumstances may be triggering physical symptoms in the first place. Below is a gift from Sadhguru himself. He has provided a link that will allow the readers of this book to learn a simple meditation called Isha Kriya: Simply type this link into your browser http://www.ishakrya.com, and become meditative.

> *"'Isha' means that which is the source of creation. 'Kriya' means an inward action towards that. Isha Kriya is a simple yet powerful tool to move from untruth to truth."*
>
> *~ Sadhguru*

Rooted in the timeless wisdom of the yogic sciences, Isha Kriya is a simple yet potent process created by Sadhguru. Lastly, aggravations plague us every day in countless ways, such as getting cut off by another driver, experiencing rudeness, etc. *Breathing* provides an elixir for this. In the words of my good friend and coach-mentor, Deb Palmer George, "every irritation is an invitation to breathe."

THE ABCs OF LIFE:

C IS FOR COMPASSION

"To practice five things under all circumstances constitutes perfect virtue; these five are gravity, generosity of soul, sincerity, earnestness, and kindness."

— *Confucius*

THE DICTIONARY DEFINES *COMPASSION* as "the deep awareness of the suffering of others coupled with the desire to relieve it." This belief guides my behavior every day. In fact, *compassion* inspired me to create my *Clear Prescriptions for Living the Life You Didn't Dream Of.* I have been through the fire, and I want to help you and as many people as possible come through your own version of the fire — unscathed.

Compassion is the virtual heartbeat of this book. I say that because one of the most powerful revelations I experienced during my 26 years as a cardiac patient is that **suffering deepens one's capacity for compassion.**

I was a *compassionate* person before my cardiac arrest. In fact, *compassion* inspired my passion for becoming a physician. However, it was only after I had suffered the physical and emotional pain, as well as depression and anxiety, that I was able to truly understand *compassion*. My own suffering enables me to first identify with people who are experiencing pain and trauma; that empathy triggers my *compassion*, an overwhelming desire to mitigate their suffering. I quantified this premise in an equation:

My deepened awareness of an agonizing condition + increased

desire to alleviate the suffering = a *compassionate* individual. The equation looks like this:

↑ AWARENESS + ↑ DESIRE = ↑ COMPASSIONATE CARE

- If you are aware of suffering, but have no desire to alleviate it, you won't be compassionate.

- If you have the desire to alleviate suffering, but cannot recognize it, you won't be compassionate.

It's important to understand the differences between sympathy, empathy, and *compassion*.

Sympathy involves feeling sorry for someone who's hurting. That feeling is somewhat emotionally detached because it comes from the point of view of an observer.

Empathy enables you to understand how someone is hurting, to the point that you almost feel their pain. It enables you to identify on a level of shared suffering by all humans.

Compassion inspires you to transform your feelings into action. *Compassion* makes you take action to help the person who is suffering, even if it means putting their needs before your own. This is a challenge for many people; that's why *The Kindness Scale* provides concrete steps that enable you to put *compassion* into action.

Some people think they are *compassionate*, but they may not be. They could be empathetic or sympathetic, but not actually *compassionate*. When you live a life of *compassion*, you are inspired by your own pain to identify with others who are enduring pain, illness, and loss. Then you channel your feelings into action.

A SPECIAL NOTE ABOUT DEVOTION:

Devotion is an extremely important component of compassion. Webster's dictionary defines it as: "the fact or state of being ardently dedicated and loyal."

This is an example of not only stepping into the shoes of another person who's suffering and having a strong desire to help them to improve their condition, but staying by their side no matter the odds of your actions influencing the outcome of their situation. True devotion will inspire you to do this even when you don't understand the circumstances.

Jeannie is the best example of a person who has totally committed herself to my well-being, which is *our* well-being. Her indomitable commitment supersedes marriage vows because in the face of a life crisis, some people cannot handle the pressure, the struggle, or the disappointment that their marriage is not the fairy tale that they envisioned on their wedding day.

A true commitment and partnership is rooted in unconditional love, which means loving a person "in sickness and in health" and selflessly devoting oneself to ensure that person's survival and success in whatever new circumstances result from the crisis at hand. Complete and unwavering devotion runs deeper than marriage. It has and continues to make a positive difference in our lives. Even today, when I experience any symptoms of my heart condition, Jeannie jumps into action as my coach and calms me down to safety. Her immense devotion inspires gratitude that I lack the words to quantify, because the love and care that she lavishes on me are so extraordinary. All the words in the dictionary could not begin to express my thankfulness to God for blessing me with Jeannie.

For Living the Life You Didn't Dream Of

Utilize the ABCs of Leadership

The ABCs of Charting a Course to a New Dream

AS MY CAREER TRAJECTORY has ascended along a new path — from solo practitioner to leadership team member in a large health-care system — I realized that the *ABCs of Life* can just as readily be applied to being a successful leader.

For example, one of today's hottest buzz phrases is "Employee Engagement." That translates into making employees feel inspired and energized about the work they do every day. I've discovered the solution: Apply the ABCs of Life to Leadership.

In doing so, think of "A" for *Acknowledgement* of your role as the leader of a team as well as the importance of others on the team. Also, *Acknowledge* the situation, circumstances, challenges, and goals of your given situation.

The successful leader rarely has to make decisions; instead, empowering the team members to make as many decisions as possible. Contrary to popular belief, the leader doesn't have the answers, but should facilitate the identification of solutions from members of the team. The ultimate form of *acknowledgement* is empowerment of those on your team.

"B" is for *Breathe* and again represents the many relaxation techniques that begin with a single, slow, deep *breath*. Leaders should always be prepared for crisis. Some believe that leadership doesn't begin until a crisis develops. By *breathing* through stressful situations, a leader can relax and allow his or her best self to shine.

Breathe passion and spiritual commitment into achieving the goal. Approach the challenge with calmness and inspire action through confidence. Specifically:

- Don't panic!

- Calm and reassure those who are in a state of panic.

- Ask the group to "take a deep *breath*."

"C" is for Commit Everyday Actions for Compassionate Living, even in the workplace. Showing *compassion* to your team builds a culture of commitment. How can you do this?

- Display *compassion* in all work that you do.

- Look for opportunities to lead by *compassionate* example.

- Acknowledge the importance of all members of the team.

- Show sincere consideration for the team and their families.

- Comment on the great contributions that members of the team are making.

- Directly ask them for their input and opinions.

CLEAR Rx #5

For Living the Life You Didn't Dream Of

Commit Everyday Actions for Compassionate Living with The Kindness Scale

"Carry out a random act of kindness, with no expectation of reward, safe in the knowledge that one day someone might do the same for you."

— *Princess Diana*

WHEN I AWAKENED TO my life's true purpose, I created a chart to outline specific acts of kindness that I can pledge to do every day to execute my life's mission to leave others better off after our interaction. I call it *The Kindness Scale*, and it takes the concept of Random Acts of Kindness to another level, which I describe as "Everyday Actions for Compassionate Living."

The Kindness Scale defines four levels of actions that you can take every day to make a positive impact on other people's lives. Those actions inevitably make you feel better, and draw positive experiences and outcomes back to you in wonderful, surprising ways.

THE KINDNESS SCALE

LEVEL I   USE BASIC GESTURES

➤ Smile.

➤ Say Hello to a stranger.

➤ Ask an injured person how they're doing.

➤ Inquire about a loved one.

➤ Compliment someone.

Level II   Take Simple Actions

➤ Offer to put a bag in the overhead bin on an airplane.

➤ Open a door for a stranger.

➤ Send an "I appreciate you" letter to a friend or colleague.

➤ When appropriate, use a gentle, comforting touch on the shoulder.

➤ Have a positive/funny spontaneous conversation with a stranger.

Level III   Take Involved Actions

➤ Use your clout to help someone.

➤ Clean up someone else's mess.

➤ Visit someone in the hospital.

➤ Pay for someone's coffee without their knowledge.

➤ Call your parents daily.

➤ Tell your spouse and kids you love them every day.

Level IV   Put Yourself at Risk

➤ Perform CPR.

➤ Donate an organ.

My daily goal is to achieve as many Level I and II activities as possible. I am always prepared to offer Level III assistance, and I consider Level IV actions depending on the circumstance.

I was inspired to create *The Kindness Scale* during an epiphany: every time I did something nice for someone, he or she smiled, laughed, exclaimed a happy "Thank you!" or simply brightened before my eyes into a happier mood. Then I recognized that my kindness created an immediate boomerang effect; it shot right back at me with a gush of good feelings because I had done something nice for someone. I quickly got hooked on this form of instant gratification!

In fact, studies show that showering others with kindness releases feel-good chemicals in your brain that are as powerful as food or drugs. This phenomenon even has a name: "Helper's High."

When making kindness a part of your daily life, your body floods with endorphins. These natural pain killers make you feel euphoric. On top of that, these mood-boosting chemicals make you healthier, help you live longer, boost your immunity, improve your relationships, boost your heart health, help you focus, reduce the stress hormone cortisol, and so much more.

And guess what? All this is FREE! It costs nothing to smile. In fact, studies show that scowling requires more muscles and energy than smiling. Likewise, you pay nothing to compliment a stranger, hold the door for someone, or share your umbrella when it's raining. As for time, these gestures can occur in a few seconds. The ancient philosopher Aesop said, "No act of kindness, no matter how small, is ever wasted."

Your split-second investment in committing an intentional act of kindness pays immeasurable dividends. I get a rush out of watching people's eyes sparkle when I give a compliment. It's delightful to witness people transform from hum-drum to happy when I surprise everyone by bringing food to the office. I feel inexplicable joy when I tell Jeannie, out of the blue, how much I appreciate her, and she beams with happiness.

Kindness makes magic happen in your life! When you do nice things for people, it has a ripple effect; they feel inspired to do something kind for other people. A study in the *New England Journal of Medicine* described this domino effect when a 28-year-old person entered a clinic, anonymously, and donated a kidney. This planned act of kindness inspired the spouses and family members of people who had received kidney donations. They, in turn, donated organs. Then, because of that one anonymous person, their donations blessed 10 people across America with new kidneys.

So how can you incorporate *The Kindness Scale* into your day? I break down each level and provide examples of how you can give and receive happy moments throughout the day.

The philosopher Sophocles said, "Kindness is ever the begetter of kindness." If every person on the planet committed to doing *Everyday Actions for Compassionate Living,* imagine what a different world this would be!

Level I

The Kindness Scale

Use Basic Gestures

The first phase of *Everyday Actions for Compassionate Living* involves your face, with expressions and words. Smile. Say "Hello" to a stranger. Ask an injured person how they're doing. Inquire about a loved one. Compliment someone. Here are some suggestions:

- Life is all about being connected to other human beings; acknowledging and making the most of these connections by sharing kind words and gestures brightens every moment.

- The elevator is one of my favorite places to do this. I find it so odd that two people can stand close to each other in a metal box for a few seconds or minutes, and not speak a word or even make eye contact. As a result, I have about 20 lines that I drop in elevators. If someone is going to a high floor, I might ask, "How's the air up there?" Or if I enter an elevator with only one person at six in the morning, I might say, "I guess we're the only ones working today." The other person chuckles, then gets chatty, and we inevitably both leave the elevator smiling, with extra pep in our steps to face the day.

- Talking about work is a safe, common ground that everyone can relate to, because everybody in the building is in the same position — at work.

- "Damn, here I am again," I often say, entering a crowded elevator. This always elicits laughter. Or at the end of the day, if I say, "Finally, we can go home," people smile and nod in agreement and chat until we reach the lobby or parking garage. Sometimes I come into work late and see people going out to lunch and I say, "One of us is going in the wrong direction!"

- It's best to refrain from conversation in awkward or inappropriate places, such as public restrooms. In addition, friendly chatter with strangers should avoid politics, religion, and sex. Weather is cliché. And not everyone is into sports. But most people *do* want to talk about their family, or their latest vacation, or how they're *really* feeling today. Before I speak, I contemplate what this person might be concerned about. And I ask myself, *What would they like to hear from me?* Since I'm sensitive about being bald, I'm careful to avoid topics that might make another person uncomfortable.

People of color, especially when they are the only two brown faces in a crowd and are often overlooked or ignored, give a quick nod to acknowledge each other. The gesture says, "I see you." I might also add, "What's up, brother?" I have learned to use this form of recognition with all people when our eyes meet.

When someone flashes a big smile, I try to approach that person and say, "Thank you for that smile. And that didn't cost anything." In most cases, they laugh, then proceed to smile at someone else, which continues a chain reaction of smiles. Every day presents countless opportunities for smiling at someone or saying something nice.

"Thank you for providing excellent customer service," you can say to the person who handled your call to the cable company.

"Have a wonderful day," you can tell the cashier at the grocery store.

It's especially rewarding when you lavish kind words on people who are often overlooked: janitors, clerks, receptionists, the barista at your favorite coffee shop, waiters and waitresses, and the list goes on. Have fun with it; savor that split-second when your kind words elicit happiness in someone who might really need a boost.

In addition to actions that reflect kindness, I regularly use "Kindness Phrases" to verbalize my gratitude to Cole, Jeannie, Mom, friends, and my closest colleagues. Here are examples of what I say every day:

- "I really appreciate you."

- "When is the last time I told you how much I appreciate you?"

- "When is the last time I told you how much I love you?"

- "Thank you, Brother." I say this to friends, colleagues and strangers alike. It creates a closeness and sense of caring since we should all love our brother.

My assistant, whose exemplary hard work and attention to detail enables me to thrive, has become delightfully accustomed to me asking, "Have I told you much I appreciate you?" Watch how much fun we have with it in the following email chain:

	To...	Williams, Herman;
Send	Cc...	
	Subject:	FW: 3 things

From:
Sent: Monday, June 13, 2016 8:06 AM
To: Williams, Herman
Subject: 3 things

   1. Good morning!
   2. I am at my desk – so whenever you arrive we can talk.
   3. All of your Quality team will be traveling this morning.
j

From: Williams, Herman
Sent: Monday, June 13, 2016 2:53 PM
To: Lorton, Jean
Subject: RE: 3 things

One thing:
Have I told you recently...

From: Lorton, Jean
Sent: Monday, June 13, 2016 2:56 PM
To: Williams, Herman
Subject: RE: 3 things

Nope - - -
But, I know you appreciate me . . . and that's a good thing!

Appreciation is contagious!

Kindness in the workplace can boost morale, productivity, and prosperity. When it comes to your friends and family, one of the most powerful ways you can express kindness is to know the power of saying, "I love you." It's extremely important to tell people how you feel, but not everyone can do that. Some are shy and get their feelings hurt, and some men think it's not manly to express emotions. I believe it's important to share how you feel when you have the opportunity, because you may never get another chance.

I always say, "I love you," to my closest male friends, including Phil. I admire him as my hero for following a spiritual path while succeeding as an actor throughout the decades since we graduated from high school. One day Phil called and said, "I admire you," then proceeded to share all the reasons why.

"Wow, I love you, man," I said. "Thanks for being in my life."

I know better than most that we never know when life could suddenly end. Doesn't it make more sense to tell the people you know and love just how much you appreciate them today, rather than risk never being able to tell them because it's too late?

With that in mind, I advocate calling your parents every day. My mother and I speak daily and text throughout the afternoon and evening. I also advise telling your spouse and kids you love them every day. You will feel overjoyed when their faces light up with happiness and warmth, so they can proceed through the day radiating love toward others.

Level II

The Kindness Scale

Take Simple Actions

Level II on *The Kindness Scale* requires you to take simple actions by physically doing something. For example, you can open a door for a stranger. Or look for opportunities in situations to help people, such as offering to put a carry-on bag in the overhead bin on an airplane. You could send an "I appreciate you" letter to a friend or colleague, or deliver a meal to a family that's enduring a health crisis or financial hardship.

If you had an outstanding meal experience at a restaurant, ask the chef to come to the table so you can personally thank him or her for the exquisite food and service. When you're happy and satisfied, let someone know.

One of my favorite Level II actions is to "Pay It Forward" by covering the cost of someone else's coffee at my favorite coffee shop. I don't even see the person's response, but I feel good thinking about the happy surprise they will feel when the cashier says that a stranger already paid for their order.

Likewise, I often give up a good parking spot if someone else is eyeing it. Or I let someone go ahead of me in the grocery line. En route to work, I give money to the man who's selling newspapers on the corner. He displays an ID for vending because he's homeless or possibly because he's been in rehabilitation for substance abuse, and selling newspapers is helping him get back on his feet.

Speaking to complete strangers or doing something kind for someone you don't know requires you to be comfortable in your own skin. It takes guts and confidence, because you risk being ignored or receiving a negative reaction. If the person fails to react in a positive manner, would that discourage you?

That points to one key to the success of *The Kindness Scale's Everyday Actions for Compassionate Living*: Don't take it personally if a person does not respond. You're not doing this for the reward. You're doing it because it enables you to make a positive contribution to help people. The odds are that the more you do this, the greater impact you will have, and it will expand exponentially through you and others.

Think of a pebble in a pond. It has a ripple effect, with each ring becoming larger and larger. The more pebbles that are dropped into the pond, the more the pond becomes covered in rings expanding outward. Writing a letter, an email, or even sending a greeting card that expresses how you feel is a great way to drop the first pebble.

LEVEL III

THE KINDNESS SCALE

TAKE INVOLVED ACTIONS

COMMITTING EVERYDAY ACTIONS FOR *Compassionate Living* from Level III of *The Kindness Scale* requires doing things that are more involved. For example, you might shovel an elderly neighbor's snow, or take him or her to the grocery store. You could also use your professional clout to help someone. For example, I love to call the nurse's station when a friend is in the hospital, and say:

"Hello, this is Dr. Herman Williams. I am Mrs. Smith's healthcare advocate. I'm calling to check on her treatment plan." (This, of course, after getting clearance from her to discuss her care.)

This has an immediate, positive impact on my friend's care — and morale — because the caregivers know someone is watching. And who has more clout in a hospital than doctors? I do that all the time, and it makes me feel great that I can positively impact a friend's level of care during his or her hospital stay.

"I'd be happy to write an intimidation factor letter," my lawyer friend says. Obviously, receiving a letter from an attorney can help to quickly resolve a conflict without expensive, time-consuming litigation. Of course, this is only appropriate when done ethically and morally.

What professional muscle can you flex to help others?

Level III *Everyday Actions for Compassionate Living* require more resources, such as time, money, and effort. Still, quick and easy actions can include cleaning up a mess that you didn't make, wiping off a bathroom counter, or picking up trash that you did not drop.

One of my favorite acts has created a legacy: I'm known for bringing bagels to the office a few times every month. This requires a plan and expenditure of resources. First, I must leave home a little earlier to stop at the bagel shop on the way to work. Then I spend my money as well as time waiting in line.

I love the significance of giving food to people I care about. Breaking bread together symbolizes sharing the sustenance of life. The office employees who may have skipped breakfast are always delighted to discover free, fresh bagels, and their expressions of joy and gratitude fill me with happiness. I love that the small investment of my time, money, and effort required to bring bagels to the office pays emotional dividends for me and so many others.

Another way you can help people on this level is to seek opportunities to uplift those experiencing misfortune. Visit someone in the hospital. Donate to a funeral fund for a stranger whose tragic death was showcased on the evening news. Volunteer at a soup kitchen.

You can also spread positive energy by writing one thank you note per week or think of the most influential people in your life, then call them to say thank you!

LEVEL IV

THE KINDNESS SCALE

PUT YOURSELF AT RISK

THE FINAL PHASE OF *The Kindness Scale* involves putting yourself at risk. For example, you can perform CPR or donate an organ. Both have the potential to save someone's life. Doing CPR can present other hazards, such as a feeling of failure if it does not work. And organ donation can threaten your own health.

However, the results can be amazing. For example, someone in my wife's Bible class donated a kidney to give a stranger the gift of life. That is the ultimate act of kindness!

For me, writing this book qualifies as *Committing Everyday Actions for Compassionate Living* at Level IV. It has required an investment of considerable resources, yet by exposing my story, I hope to help countless people around the world who take the time to read my story. The risk involves making myself vulnerable or being criticized. Perhaps that's why it's taken me 26 years to write this book. At first, my message simply did not seem powerful enough. But every time I told the story, people exclaimed, "Oh my God! You *have* to write a book!"

As I matured, after the stroke, I was consumed with gratitude that God had helped me recover from another major health crisis. With that came the realization that my story is not merely about survival. It is about purpose. It pushed me to do something, regardless of the odds, to shift my focus to three things:

1. Accept what has happened to me, and where I am now.

2. Meditate to discover the meaning of what happened, and the purpose it has provided for how I live today.

3. Pinpoint my purpose in life and understand how to use it to help myself and others.

Now, will you commit to using *The Kindness Scale* in your daily life? How many *Everyday Actions for Compassionate Living* will you pledge to take? Use the chart below to track what you're doing, as well as the responses. Note which actions elicit the best responses, and as a result, merit repeated use.

Track Your Everyday Actions for Compassionate Living

Date	Act of Kindness	Level	Recipient	Their Response	Your Response	Outcome

These all turn compassion into some level of action and can make all the difference in the world when practiced with regularity. Throughout the day, keep in mind that every person you encounter is dealing with some issue, whether small or big. A gesture of kindness can improve their mood, and therefore their condition. I witness this every day on my way to work, at lunch, in the store, and in airports across America. The power of kindness is immeasurable; take action today to share the magic!

> *"The most beautiful people we have known are those who have known defeat, known suffering, known struggle, known loss, and have found their way out of those depths."*
>
> — *Elisabeth Kubler-Ross*

How Do You Make A New Dream?

When your dream dies during a health crisis, a divorce, a family tragedy, or some other catastrophe, you must seek alternatives. This requires soul-searching.

What other role can you play in the world that draws upon your talents and abilities right now? Amazingly, the Master's degree in Public Health (MPH) that I earned in conjunction with my MD had — without my intention — laid the foundation to prepare me for my new dream, which is my current career. This is further evidence that a Higher Power was preparing me for a life purpose about which I had absolutely no idea at the time. My reasons for pursuing an MPH had — as far as I knew at the time — nothing to do with the fact that someday I would be forced to abandon my dream of becoming an orthopedic surgeon.

Are you nurturing another skill that you could spin into a whole new career? It may be a hobby, or a passion. Dare to dream huge, new dreams, while also looking at smaller goals. The person who dreamed of being a concert pianist, but became paralyzed, can become a music producer. He or she could also use that knowledge to teach. Don't be defined by what you cannot do. Think about new things that you *can* do.

While *The Kindness Scale* focuses on doing nice things for other people, it must start with being kind to yourself and loving yourself first. Acceptance of your situation, which includes being gentle and patient with your adjustment to life after a crisis — this is the first major step on the journey. Know that you have value, and that by embracing the possibilities of a new future, you can serve as a catalyst for someone else.

Your dream is your mission. When you have a mission, you feel fulfilled and happier about life. We're all here to help each other by improving each other's lives. That's the mission of compassion. I'm here to improve the lives of others, which will improve my life.

One of the most celebrated examples of someone discovering his life purpose during a potentially deadly crisis was Captain Chesley Burnett "Sully" Sullenberger, who landed US Airways Flight 1549 in the Hudson River off Manhattan on January 15, 2009. All 155 people on board survived. Captain Sully declared during a presentation I attended, that he felt he was "born" to perform that miraculous feat that day and save the lives of those 155 passengers.

Our job is to discover what we were born to do. In doing so, we can impart to others that everyone's role is to be compassionate and kind to each other. Even better, sharing the message that if you feel your life is lacking, you can begin receiving by first giving.

You will forever warm the hearts of people whom you lavished with kindness and love. The late author and poet Maya Angelou summed it up best by saying, "Your legacy is every life you have touched."

I invite you right now to begin building a life legacy of purpose and joy by applying my Clear Prescriptions for Living the Life You Didn't Dream Of.

Appendix

Eulogy for Herman Johnny Williams — Father to Herman Joseph Williams

TODAY I DON'T JUST shed tears that my father's life is over; I celebrate that it happened...

In a world where many men mourn the absence of a living father... I celebrate the legacy of a Father that will never end. I can only thank God that in a world where many Black men are torn and depressed because they never experienced a Father who affirmed or loved them... Today I celebrate with much gratitude and humility; a father who started early in my life affirming and loving me and continued doing so until his last hours.

In a world where many men have had to watch the torment of seeing their mother disrespected by their Father... I had the privilege of watching my dad celebrate my mom daily for 62 years. My dad gave me direction, confidence, and motivation at times when I really needed it. Whether he was showing me the beauty of classical music or instilling in me a sense of academic accomplishment by buying my one-year-old son an alumni chair from Amherst College. He impacted and shaped my life. He showed me that action wins over planning to act and that strength does not come from physical capacity... it comes from the development of character, integrity, and a sense of purpose.

I can look back now and remember scenes that played themselves out many times with my dad as I was growing up.... Like the fact that he never missed a basketball or football game of mine (even though I wasn't any good in either sport). He never missed a track meet or a music recital of mine... He was just simply there for me all the time. Like many other people, he could be stubborn and didn't do his exercises at home. However, he currently holds the record for the oldest person to have completed the Kaiser Pulmonary rehab program.

I always knew the talks we had throughout my life were not lectures, but an investment in my future.... Priceless knowledge that many men search for throughout their entire life. I had a father who knew the value of life lessons. He made sure he taught me, and today I stand as a Man who received every word. As many of you know, he was a funny man. He joked until his last days of consciousness. I can remember about two weeks ago, he called me close to his bed and whispered:

"I asked God to take me out of this world and he wouldn't do it. I woke up and I'm still here."

To which I replied, "Dad, it isn't your time yet."

To which he replied, "Maybe he's just busy!"

My dad built a strong foundation in me that I can never forget or take for granted. I truly thank God for the priceless gift of a man who knew the essence of what it meant to be an exemplary husband and father. I pray every day that I can be half the father to my son that my dad was to me. He is the benchmark for me and was for many of my friends.

Life for all of us is the sum of the choices that we make... today I celebrate my dad's choices... He chose to walk as a man of character and integrity... He chose to love and honor his family... Today I am positively impacted by those choices... and I will forever love and cherish the memory of my dad, Herman Williams.

Mom, I will be there for you and will not leave you alone.

Thank you all.

Photo by Chad Driver

Herman J. Williams MD Biography

HERMAN J. WILLIAMS, MD, is the chief clinical officer for RegionalCare Capella Health (RCCH) Healthcare Partners. In this role, he oversees all quality, safety, and clinical activities for the company's 17 regional health systems in 13 states. These include hospitals in Alabama, Arizona, Arkansas, Connecticut, Idaho, Iowa, Montana, Ohio, Oklahoma, Oregon, South Carolina, Texas, and Washington.

Dr. Williams has a specialized expertise in public health and policy issues, and works with physicians and clinicians across large healthcare systems.

He received a Master of Public Health degree in Health Policy and Management from Harvard University School of Public Health in Boston, Massachusetts in1987. Graduating with honors, Williams earned his Doctor of Medicine degree from Boston University School of Medicine in Boston, Massachusetts, in 1988, and a Master of Business Administration from the Foster School of Business at the University of Washington in Seattle, Washington, in 2004.

A professional certified coach (PCC) in the International Coach Federation, Dr. Williams applies professional coaching to focus on setting goals, creating outcomes, and managing personal change.

For the past 26-years, he has been married to Jeannie Williams, a retired dental hygienist. The couple has one son, Cole, who is 21.